how to make it in

# HOLLYWOOD

★ ★ ★ ★ ★ ★ ★ ★ ★ ★ ★ ★ ★ ★ ★ ★ ★ ★ ★ ★ ★ ★ ★ ★ ★ ★ ★ ★

# how to make it in
# HOLLYWOOD

★ ★ ★ ★ ★ ★ ★ ★ ★ ★ ★ ★ ★ ★ ★ ★ ★ ★ ★ ★ ★ ★ ★ ★ ★ ★ ★ ★

Wende Hyland
and
Roberta Haynes

**Nelson-Hall nh Chicago**

**Library of Congress Cataloging in Publication Data**

Hyland, Wende.
    How to make it in Hollywood.

    1. Moving-pictures as a profession.    2. Acting as
a profession.    I. Haynes, Roberta, joint author.
II. Title.
PN1995.9.P75H9        791.43ʟ092ʟ2        75-17523
ISBN 0-88229-239-0

Manufactured in the United States of America

# Contents

# Preface

This book is written for, and dedicated to, that vast army of hopefuls—some talented, some not so talented—who yearn to face a camera or an audience. It is also for anyone who has ever seen a movie, watched television, or seen a play and is curious about that fascinating phenomenon, the person driven to be an actor.

In a series of interviews with some of the outstanding people in the film world you will discover how an actor gets his first break, how he gets through that "iron door," why some succeed while others, perhaps more talented, fail. You will also meet some of the people who control the actor's destiny.

Without the actor there is no film. Yet, to a great extent in the beginning, the actor is the one who is stepped on, pushed around, and many times ignored. His talent, the very thing that makes him unique, is not always his most valuable asset. In fact, talent can sometimes be a hindrance.

The people interviewed in this book all agree that to become a star one must have a certain X factor, but not everyone agrees on the definition of X. All do agree, however, that without it, although the actor may be steadily employed, he can never reach stardom. But the big question is, how does one get started? How does one get that "lucky break"? What is the secret? Is it talent, beauty, sex appeal, luck, timing, or just what?

The following interviews, transcribed from tapes, are in question-and-answer form. We determined to preserve the ad-lib, straight-from-the shoulder quality of these conversations by avoiding polishing or rewriting by press agents or outsiders. Some of the questions for which you will find answers in the following chapters are:

1. What do film executives look for when they cast a film or television show?

2. What does the actor feel when he goes on an interview, and how does he cope with that horror— rejection?

3. What is the producer's role compared to that of executive producer, and what are their various functions?

4. Does the director really cast the film or television show? If so, what is the function of the casting director?

5. How valuable are the years and years of training in legitimate theater? Does stage work impress most people in film and television?

6. Just why and how did such actors as Jack Lemmon and Walter Matthau reach the top? Does an actor of their caliber really feel that he's "made it"?

7. What would Jack Lemmon do today if he were just starting out?

8. Do actors really feel "fulfilled" once they've become successful?

9. What is the agent's function? What is he supposed to do toward building an actor's career?

10. How does an unknown actor find an agent, and what kind of agent is best for him? If the actor doesn't have an agent, is it difficult for him to get to see anybody in the business?

11. How did Albert S. Ruddy get to be producer of *The Godfather?* What was his background?

12. How did Aaron Spelling move from acting to being one of the biggest television producers in Hollywood?

13. Why has Lee Marvin been with his agent, Meyer Mishkin, for over twenty years when most actors change agents every other year or so?

14. Is there a certain formula for success?

# Jack Lemmon

## Actor

"I'm hopeful that between the ages of fifty and sixty
I'm going to be a hell of an actor."

Jack Lemmon, born in Boston on February 8, 1925, prepared at Andover and graduated from Harvard. He served as a communications officer with the rank of ensign aboard the carrier *Champlain*. After the navy his next stop was New York, where he made his debut on Broadway in a revival of *Room Service*. From there he was called to Hollywood. In 1955 he won an Oscar for *Mister Roberts* and became a star, and in 1967 he received the Laurel Award as the number one box office star. In 1971 he directed the feature film *Kotch*, starring his friend Walter Matthau. In 1973 Jack Lemmon won the Academy Award as best actor for his role in *Save the Tiger*, an award for which he had been nominated three times before.

## Films

*It Should Happen to You*
*Three for the Show*
*Phffft!*
*My Sister Eileen*
*Mister Roberts*
*You Can't Run Away from It*
*Fire Down Below*
*Operation Mad Ball*
*Cowboy*
*Bell, Book and Candle*
*It Happened to Jane*
*Some Like It Hot*
*The Apartment*
*The Wackiest Ship in the Army*
*The Notorious Landlady*
*Days of Wine and Roses*

*Irma La Douce*
*Under the Yum Yum Tree*
*Good Neighbor Sam*
*How to Murder Your Wife*
*The Great Race*
*The Fortune Cookie*
*Luv*
*The Odd Couple*
*The April Fools*
*The Out of Towners*
*The War Between Men and Women*
*Avanti*
*Save the Tiger*
*The Front Page*
*The Prisoner of Second Avenue*

Jack Lemmon's company, Jalem Productions, is in the center of Beverly Hills. It is tastefully decorated but is without that "decorator's touch." We arrived right at 11:30, the time of our appointment. He wasn't there but thoughtfully called from his home to say that he was just leaving and would be there in five minutes. He was. He ambled in, apologizing for being a little the worse for wear from the night before. He was dressed undeliberately and casually, and he puffed on a large cigar. He introduced himself and immediately charmed us. He's an extremely attractive man, both in looks and in personality. It's easy to see why Jack Lemmon is a star.

● *If you were a young actor starting out today, how would you go about it?*

I think there's only one way—through schools and colleges. Within the last decade or the last fifteen years the colleges have really expanded in the performing, interpretive, and creative arts. Some of these schools are sensational. Then, once you've finished with that— God Almighty, I don't know. Fortunately, I have never been in that position of coming out to Hollywood and searching. When I did come out, it was because they asked me to. Also, that was twenty years ago, and all I know is that it's tougher now because the "studio system" no longer exists. In other words, people aren't under contract to a studio anymore, so the only thing you can do is hopefully get an agent, get in a play, get seen.

● *How did you get seen?*

I got lucky, and I was born at the right time. When I was through with my education, I went to New York. It was in the mid-forties. I starved for a couple of years, which is nothing. Finally I was able to get a few auditions for soap operas and got a couple of running parts. It gave me maybe thirty dollars a week on an average. Hell, I could live on five at that time. But the main thing was being at the right place at the right time. Television was just emerging, just starting. Worthington Minor, producer of "Studio One," didn't even have a door on his office because CBS was expanding so rapidly, and I was able to get in. Next thing I knew, I had a part on the show "Shadow of a Gunman." I told them I was from Ireland, with the Abbey Players. Chuck Heston and I both got twenty-five dollars for eight days' work. Somebody saw me, and the next thing you know, I had another part. Then Sidney Lumet saw something, then

Frankenheimer and Arthur Penn. I was doing "Web" and "Suspense," et cetera.

I did four or five hundred shows in about five years—all kinds of parts—and I had that great good fortune of being around when there were no stars in a new medium. Today . . . what does a kid do? That's a very difficult problem. George Burns had the definitive line a few years ago. He said the biggest problem is there's no place for a kid to be lousy anymore. We don't have repertory like England does, and it's very, very difficult.

● *Was there ever a period in your acting career when you wanted to throw it all in and do something else?*

Not really. I think there's a marvelous thing about youth—blind stupidity. That's what keeps you going. If someone says, "There is one chance in a million that you'll ever be able to make a living, let alone be as successful as you would like," the kid who wants to act says, "Oh, that's all right; I'll make it." He just goes right on. I was that way. It never dawned on me that I wouldn't. You have to have that. In retrospect, it scares the hell out of me. As lucky as I was, I still can't figure it all out. I just assumed it was going to happen and it did. I worked hard and I still do. I don't find the acting process easy. I beat a part to death with a stick.

● *Did you study acting in New York?*

Only after I had already had experience. I worked in some study classes with professionals taught by Uta Hagen and then with David Alexander. He was terrific! One of the things he really concentrated on was the fact that actors were faced ninety percent of the time with bad material. He taught us to work with obstacles and counterpoint, anything we could to make dull scenes much more interesting. I found this enormously advantageous to me. It really made me think instead of just taking the first literal interpretation. In other words, what do you select to play, never really being satisfied.

● *What made you want to be an actor?*

I've often wondered myself. As far back as I can remember, I wanted to be an actor. Several things probably make people want to be actors. The obvious is the desire for attention—"Look at me, Mommy; look at me, Daddy." Well, if you heighten that a little above the norm, maybe you have the seeds of a personality that wants to be an actor. It's one of the obvious ways to get attention.

I imagine that was within me, but I think accidents happen too. For instance, one suddenly finds out he has a talent for it. You happen to do a play at school; suddenly you get a laugh; suddenly you hear applause—you've pleased people. Well, that's the beginning. That's what happened to me. I replaced somebody in a play at school. I was about six or seven and had three pages of dialogue but certainly couldn't learn it, and so the teacher sat on the side of the stage. I remember I had a big, wide hat and a black cape and was supposed to be an old man. I went on, walked all the way over to the side of the stage; she gave me my line, and I walked back to the middle, said the line, and proceeded to walk back to the side of the stage again, where she told me my next line. And I repeated this process through the whole three pages. I got enormous roars of laughter because it was quite obvious what was happening. The laughs just kept getting bigger and bigger and, well, there was no way. . . . I can still remember it vividly to this very day, and I'm now forty-nine—it's over forty years ago.

I think an interesting thing, though: I do feel some people become actors because they hate being themselves and they want to be somebody else. They really come to life when they are somebody else—they're usually very good actors. Now that doesn't mean if you are a good actor that's necessarily true; I hope it doesn't apply to me. But I've seen actors like that, and you can tell it in their eyes. The minute the curtain drops they fall back into themselves, their own guilts, their own neuroses, et cetera. But, my God, when that curtain goes up they're somebody else; it's the only thing that keeps them alive emotionally.

So many people think actors are nuts, they're emotional babies, and that acting basically is not an emotionally stable thing. I think exactly the opposite. I think it's as healthy as hell. One of the reasons why people are a little in awe of actors is because they would love to do exactly what actors do. Instead of having to talk to themselves in the closet or the mirror and be Walter Mitty, actors are allowed to do it; they're able to live out these fantasies and get paid for it. A lot of actors would be absolute emotional basket cases if they weren't able to act. They really need to do it more than the norm.

● *Do you have any desire to go back to the stage?*

Yes; I love it. It's one of the most rewarding areas for an actor for two obvious reasons. One, you give a sustained performance; and two, you have a live audience, which, of course, you can't get in film. In film you can fall into bad habits. You can forget and end up unconsciously falling back on personal mannerisms and things that are comfortable, and you can do this unconsciously, no matter how much experience you've had, especially if you have a director who doesn't catch it. And then, very often that's what they want. They want a Jack Lemmon performance or they want a Walter Matthau performance—whatever the hell that is.

● *Do people still see you in "Jack Lemmon-type" roles?*
Sure; very often. I get a flock of them that are "Jack Lemmon" scripts. Usually they'll be comedies, and usually they're surface. I think comedy is harder to write, especially comedy that has any real meaning— not that it always has to have meaning. *Some Like It Hot* was pure farce, and I adore farce. But it's awfully hard to write, and there are very few directors who can do it.

● *When you first came to Hollywood, you were one of the few young comedians who could play romantic comedy. Why is there nobody today?*
I don't know why, but there never really has been a lot and how I got in it I don't know. It just happened. The first part I had was in a film with Judy Holliday, *Phffft!,* which was a romantic comedy. They pigeonhole you anyway, and so, because that was successful, the next thing you know, ninety percent of the scripts that I got were comedies, which was the reason I ended up doing comedy. In New York, although I did comedy and got a lot of experience in it, I also did just as many dramas.

● *But so few young actors do comedy today.*
It's true and I don't know why; I'm damned if I do. Of course, there are times when I'm glad! I'd been here

9

about four years when I picked up the morning trades*
and someone at Paramount said, "We've found a young
Jack Lemmon." I said, "Holy God!"

● *Do you think Los Angeles is the only place where the actor
gets the opportunity to break into film and television?*

It's difficult anywhere. The theater in New York is in a
terrible state. We've been saying that for the past thirty
years, but it's true. Off-Broadway and off-off-Broadway
are the only reasons it still exists, and the chances of
getting a part, no matter how small, in a Broadway play
are as remote as hell unless you've been seen in other
productions somewhere. But theater is the most
important place to learn what you're doing. Any kid
who wants to be discovered, wants to be a "movie star,"
is insane, absolutely crazy, and is living a dream. The
so-called days of being found at Schwab's Drug Store
are gone. Those things *did* happen to a very small
extent years ago because they went more on beauty.

When I first came out in fifty-five, there were still
some kids that were being pushed and groomed for
stardom before they even knew what the hell acting was
all about. You cannot learn the acting process in film
without spending years and years, because film, of
necessity, is done in bits and pieces, and you never get to
give any real kind of sustained performance. You say a
few lines and someone says, "Cut"; then they pick it up
and you've never done the scene before. Two weeks later
you're doing the beginning of the film, and you've
already shot the end. It's terribly difficult, and I've seen
kids who just couldn't take it.

---

*Newspapers of the film and television industries. Examples are *Hollywood
Reporter* and *Variety*.

Tony Curtis learned how to act mostly in film, and my hat is off to him. He learned by really applying himself in those rotten things when he was a beautiful young kid with a lot of curly hair and they shoved him into those things at Universal with swords and everything—"Yonder lies the castle of my father" and all that. But he really cared and tried to learn the process of acting. It took twenty years, because he hadn't the experience before he was playing big parts, didn't know what the hell acting was all about, but he learned under the most impossible circumstances. I believe the most secure actors are the ones that really only wanted to be the best actors—not "stars"—that takes care of itself.

● *How do you feel about television? Do you think you will ever do any yourself?*

I might, but it would be because I was having trouble getting features. As long as I can make a living doing features, I would prefer it. God knows I make enough bad pictures, but your chances of doing something good on television are about a hundred to one because of the economic necessities. You have to shoot three or four times as much per day. If you walk in front of a camera, they're apt to print it; if you're fifteen feet away from the camera, you're in a close-up. You don't get the rehearsals, and you don't get the number of takes. You really don't get the time to dig and get what you can in a feature. You also can't do the material you can do in a feature. If I ever tried to do *Save the Tiger* for television, they'd cut one-third of it out. You're not selling the movie in television; you're selling a product. It has to appeal to the lowest common denominator and try not to offend anybody. In general, I feel anything really good is an individual statement, and you can't begin to worry about offending anybody. You have to let the creative people do it their way and hope that enough people will agree with them. That's very difficult in television.

● *As a director, have you worked with young people? How do you feel about them? Do you believe they know their craft?*

I love working with young people. I really haven't done that much direction. I've done one feature and some direction on the stage, a bit in television, and the film *Kotch* with Walter Matthau, who's superb. There was a kid in that, Deborah Winters, who had good quality, but she was floundering to an extent, purely from lack of experience. How much talent she has is impossible to tell. You never really *can* tell until someone has the chance to get the right part and suddenly they open up. They get that security, that professional security, that maturity, and suddenly they reach that plateau where they don't worry about exposing anything. They just let it all hang out, and who knows how far they can go?

The big problem in acting is not just getting the job. The problem is getting a good part in a good company with a good director and, until then, you'll never know how good you might be or if you're good enough to be a working, viable, professional actor. You can have worked for ten years before that ever happens.

● *Do you think a good actor can perform badly due to mediocre direction?*

I do, especially in the medium of film. There's no question that film is the director's medium; he's in total control, including the editing. I was terribly aware, in comedy especially, of what editing can do. An actor can time lines and beats, but those beats can be taken out by a director who's tone-deaf or who doesn't have that sense of rhythm. Instead of letting you take a long beat,

which is the only reason why a line suddenly becomes
funny, he takes the beat out and you can pick up the cue
at the wrong time. A couple of times I was outraged at
seeing myself in a film and suddenly seeing a reaction
that was put in a different place; I'm suddenly doing a
take on something that I did on another line, but they
put it back on another one because they thought it was
funny. Mainly it bothered me because I never really did
it that way. It was not my performance, and I felt it was
illegitimate. I felt raped.

● *Who is one of the most exciting directors you've worked
with?*

Probably the most exciting . . . Billy Wilder. That's
also because we're so close personally that it overlaps.
I'm prejudiced because it's been such a joy to work with
him. We're on the same wavelength at this point; after
five films he doesn't even direct me. He just starts to say
something, and I know what he means. It's that old
chemistry thing. It happens with actor and actor, and
also actor and director. When I work with Walter
Matthau, there's nothing to it—it just flows and we
have a ball. Two very fine actors may have great
difficulty working together because somehow they're
not on that same wavelength, don't communicate with
each other. And a fine director can have great trouble
with some actors because he, also, can't communicate,
and they keep fishing to find each other. That's
difficult.

● *Do you believe that it is vital for everyone connected with a
film to know each other, have a certain rapport, good
communication?*

Very definitely. One of the biggest problems, and something which really threw me at first, was the fact that
ninety-nine out of a hundred films start shooting

without rehearsal. You walk on and you meet the cast, and two hours later you're doing a scene with them as opposed to getting to know them so you can really act *with* them instead of just *at* them. Ninety-nine percent of the actors just act *at;* they don't act *with.* And this is the biggest problem. I think that they're learning the lines and saying the words, and when someone says, "Listen!" to the other actor, they think it means listening to the words. That has nothing to do with it. You don't listen to words, per se; we try to listen to what the person means underneath. We're not even that conscious of the words we use. I'm not conscious of the words I'm using now; I'm conscious of trying to get a thought across. When actors *really* work together, they're listening to the person, not the words.

● *Have there been any roles you really found difficult?*

Yes; oh, yes. Absolutely. *Tiger* I found difficult and *Wine and Roses* because of the emotional involvement. There's no way that you shut the office door at six and forget it till the next morning. That's an impossible thing—for some people more than others—for me *especially.* Walter Matthau, I know, finds the acting process much simpler than I do. He works a different way, and he's able to handle it with less personal involvement and yet give a marvelous performance.

● *Isn't he playing different kinds of parts from those you play, though?*

It would depend. But say there was a part that we could both play, we'd both be right for, even though we're quite different. Walter would probably have less trouble and give just as good or better a performance, with less emotional involvement—personal involvement—because I get all screwed up in it and go through hell; I really do. The acting process to me is delicious hell. I love it; I adore it; but I find it very difficult.

● *What do you feel about method acting, where people sit around discussing each line, dissecting everything?*

I think it's just dandy. I think you can analyze a part and blah, blah, blah just as long as two things don't happen. Don't overanalyze it or analyze it to death, forgetting the real reason why you're there, why an actor is ever there; and two, as long as you aren't unconsciously or consciously looking to make the part comfortable, to make it for you, to bend it to where you feel secure. Because you're feeling good in a scene doesn't mean anything. It's what the audience feels, not what *you* feel. There are times when I've done a scene—and I know this applies to any actor—when the director will say, "Print," and you say, "You've got to be kidding! It was absolutely god-awful; I wasn't in it; I lost my concentration; it felt terrible! Can I do another one?" He says, "OK, sure," and after a few more you finally say, "Gee, that was good; print that one!" You go to the rushes, you look at them, and he was dead right—the other one was much better.

It doesn't necessarily have a damn thing to do with what you feel, but a lot of actors are so involved with how *they* feel. They think if they feel a scene the audience is going to feel it, but if that were true you could turn upstage, mutter, and absolutely get lost in the character. In the meantime, the audience is fleeing the theater because it's dull as hell. There's only one reason why an actor is on stage: to be getting the highest possible level of dramatic conflict within the scene and to be carrying out the author's intent. A lot of actors

15

work terribly hard figuring out what they *can* do, as opposed to what they *should* do, and the more you act the more you realize that. Really good actors begin more and more to think like directors; they begin to think of the overall of the scene and not just what they can do with it. I love watching Gene Hackman because he has the ability to make you feel it's really happening for the first time, that he's not just spouting out lines from his mouth—almost as if he's ad-libbing.

● *Do you feel fulfilled in your career as an actor?*

No. But I will admit, in general, I'm very happy. With all the frustrations that anyone is going to have in any career, I *am* happy, because overall I've been fortunate enough to be in some terrific films and have some absolutely marvelous parts. And some of them I've done pretty well. The biggest problem I have is the age-old one of trying to be the best actor you can be—not the best actor in the world, but the best actor *you* can be.

● *Is it more satisfying for you to do dramatic roles?*

Not necessarily. The greatest part I've ever done was *Save the Tiger,* and not because it was a drama; it was the part. I loved *Some Like It Hot* in its way—that was such a dippy, crazy nut—and *Wine and Roses,* a heavy, heavy drama. I loved that. It really just depends on the part itself.

I'm forty-nine and realize that hopefully between fifty and sixty I'm going to be a hell of an actor. When you asked me whether I was satisfied with my career and I said, "Yes, overall," it was because I've never had the straight leading man crap. Although I am a leading man, they're really character parts. The leading man-type role is limited, written straight, and I never got stuck with that, thank God. As I get older I feel it will only get better and better. You get into those rich character parts, which are what I've always wanted. And from fifty to sixty, if you're still healthy and have the energy to play anything, no matter how demanding the part, you're older, more mature, and your craft and technique should be at their peak.

● *Who has been one of the most exciting women you have worked with?*

Judy Holliday. She was the best actress.

● *Did you ever get close to Marilyn Monroe?*

We were very good friends, but I never got close to her. Very few people ever did. She was obviously very unhappy, and she'd let you get just so near and then withdraw because she didn't want to be hurt anymore. She'd been hurt an awful lot. Obviously, certain people were much closer to her than I was, but we got along very, very well. There was just so far I could go, and then she'd cut off.

● *Was she an instinctive actress?*

Totally. I think she was sensational in one respect. She was a goddamn good comedienne, and when I say she was instinctive it doesn't mean she didn't know what she was doing. What was uncanny was how much she *did* know. The greatest talent that Marilyn had was the ability to use the talents that she had *completely*, and that in itself is a rare talent. Most actors can't use all their talents no matter how good they are. They never tap it all. She had an unbelievable instinct of what was right for her. She would never wait for Billy Wilder to say, "Cut." She would suddenly say, "Stop, stop." The scene may have been going fine, but not for her.

She really didn't act with you; she couldn't. That's not the kind of actress she was. In *Some Like It Hot* we once did thirty-five or thirty-six takes in which she had seven words in a particular scene. She had to come into the room and say, "Where's the bourbon? . . . Oh, there it is." She wouldn't complete the two lines until they were right *for her*. Billy was going crazy. At about take thirty-three or thirty-five they had tried eighteen different ways to get it out of her. About take thirty-five, when it was just about going to be done again, Billy said, "We can't possibly—" and Marilyn said, "Ssh, don't talk to me or I'll forget how I want to play it." I fell over. But, good for her, she knew what she wanted, and she was damned if she was going to let Billy have that film until it was right. Then she'd turn around and do three pages in one take! Scare the hell out of you.

● *It must have been difficult working with her.*

In that sense, yes. Yet it was very exciting. Sometimes you'd look at her playing a scene and swear she wasn't doing anything at all. After, when you'd go to the rushes, you'd never look at yourself; all you'd do is stare at this girl, because something happened between her and that lens. It may not have come from her to you, but it sure as hell went from her to that lens. She really was unique . . . something else. There's a certain thing that can happen on film with some people. Betty Grable had it; you just looked at her. Marlon has it; he has it both on stage and film. He has that chemistry that doesn't happen often. It's rather rare, to say the least.

● *How do you feel about being a great star or celebrity? Does it affect your private life?*

Not a hell of a lot. I think there's a certain ego satisfaction in people paying attention to you. Why the hell were you an actor in the first place? If they're not paying attention to you, you're through. Brando runs away from it, and Jimmy Cagney, a totally different personality, couldn't wait to retire. And that's great—that's fine—to each his own. But an actor has to realize it's part and parcel of his career. An actor can't say, "Don't pay attention to me," and then say, "What's my next part?" because it just doesn't work that way.

It bothers me mostly if I'm in a restaurant and someone comes roaring up. Then all of a sudden there are twenty people, and there goes your steak. But, what the hell, that's no big deal! I'm really pleased and flattered but still feel a little self-conscious when I sense everybody's looking at me.

● *Do you think it's important for an actor to have publicity today?*

More important is what kind of publicity; I think *that* is extremely important. Marlon, for instance, can get more coverage than anyone else by refusing to do *any* publicity, so they write like mad about him. So, it can even work that way. It can be terribly valuable, but it depends on how and what you do.

● *What importance do you put on education?*

It's absolutely vital. Every now and then you get that age-old question thrown at you—some kid who has finally and firmly made up his mind that he wants to be an actor and wonders why the hell he should spend another four years completing his education when he could be concentrating on acting. An overall education is the most beneficial thing he can possibly get. Anything that broadens his horizon will make him a better actor, better equipped to face any kind of part, because he doesn't know what kind of part he's going to be faced with—that's if he's lucky enough to face any. Long before I went to Harvard, I wanted to be an actor and at times I thought, "What in hell am I doing here?" Well, I was there because there was a war on; I had no choice. But even then I thought, "What am I doing studying this and that? I want to act, and I have little time for anything else. I have to concentrate on what I really want to do." But everything I was taking—and I don't care if it was Rock Throwing in the Middle Ages—helped me.

● *What influences your wanting to play a particular role in a script?*

I think that unconsciously you're influenced à la *Tiger*. For instance, that script not only appealed to me as an actor as a hell of a part, but also I felt it was saying something and that the biggest problem we have is not just that a Watergate can happen but that we condone it. That's as bad as the fact that morally, ethically, our ideals are gone—the age of innocence is gone. Instead of saying, "How could you?" it becomes, "Well, do you think you can get away with it?" That's why I felt the picture had something, because it could make you think a little. We all are like ostriches; we just keep our heads stuck in the sand. We're so worried about our own personal problems that we don't think very often of the whole, overall ills of our society. We tend to just forget instead of doing something about it. So I do think I'm influenced in that sense, not just by the part, but the content of the script.

# Tony Spinner

## Television Producer

"It has nothing to do with acting, in fact, acting can be a detriment."

Tony Spinner was born in New York on April 4, 1930. He completed his education at Syracuse and Hofstra Universities. After graduation he started writing and became executive story editor for the well-known "Matinee Theatre." He was nominated for an Emmy for his teleplay "All the Hoffmeyers in the World," which he wrote for "Matinee Theatre."

Since coming to Hollywood he has written for television and produced the following shows:

"The Dakotas"
"The Man from UNCLE"
"The Invaders"
"Dan August"
"Mod Squad"
"Search"
"The FBI"
"Cannon"
"Caribe"

We interviewed Tony Spinner at his home in Beverly Hills on a Saturday morning, two hours before he was leaving for the race track. He and his wife were downing coffee in the kitchen. There seemed to be the usual Saturday morning pandemonium—noises everywhere, mostly from their daughter and her playmate. We were finally enclosed in the living room and got from Tony one of the most honest, candid interviews we have had about the television industry—no holds barred. Somewhat embittered, frustrated, but resigned to what the television industry and Hollywood has become, he seems to say, "It's all bullshit. Give me my money and my Saturday at the track."

- *When producers and directors say they're looking for new talent, do you think it's true?*

It might be true in features, but it's certainly not true in television. If you have to cast a seventeen-year-old girl who is supposed to be the most astonishing-looking woman in the world and who acts like Ethel Barrymore, yeah, maybe you'll see new people because you're desperate, but as long as you're not desperate, as long as you can sit down and make up a cast list and name fifty people—known people—for each show, no.

While I was doing "Search," I *never* saw people. Jimmy Merrick, the casting man, and I would sit down together. If you're smart, you ignore the directors, because either they're trying to get laid or they don't know anything. So Jimmy Merrick and I would cast the entire show in twenty minutes. It was just a question of "Is Patrick O'Neal available? Is Harry Guardino available?" We'd have our one, two, threes; we'd get on the phone and half the show would be cast. The network would be very happy to see Patrick O'Neal in a show and be delighted to have Rhonda Fleming as she has a name, even though she can't act at all, but she's a nice lady. You go through it right like that.

We weren't interested in new people; you don't have time for that. You're doing a show every seven days, and the minute you get through one, you're doing another and the scripts are coming in for the next ten; writers' meetings are backed up—you can't believe it. Who's got time to go on a talent hunt? I'm used to casting a show between five and seven o'clock. I don't have weeks to start looking at actors, and if a director says, "I don't want him," I'm ready to hit him in the mouth because that means I'm going to have to see people. There are very few people you can't get. For instance, you can't get Charlie Bronson—although five years ago you could have bought him for a quarter. You can't get Lee Marvin, Paul Newman, or Bobby Redford, but you can get most of the rest.

● *So you feel the chance for a young actor without any credits is almost impossible in television?*

Yes, because the first question anybody asks is, "Have you any film?" and if you hear there's no film and it's a crowded day, the chances of my seeing the actor are very, very small. A day like I had yesterday—as producer of a TV show, was so incredibly busy I didn't even have a chance to eat. You're not about to stop, like on a motion picture, and say, "OK, I'll see him (or her)." You're just gonna say, "Hey, forget it." There was a rare example yesterday. An agent sent this girl out. She was very beautiful, blah, blah, blah, and the casting lady said, "Will you meet her?" She came and talked for one minute, you could tell she had no training, no background, and immediately your mind is drifting off to your next problem. It's almost impossible.

● *Do your directors ever want to use specific actors they've seen in theater?*

I haven't met too many directors who wanted to use somebody they've seen in theater out here, but perhaps someone they've seen in another TV show or a movie or maybe a New York actor. My attitude is kind of resigned—"OK, if you insist"—but the chances of that person getting the job are minimal because if you're dealing with the producer of a television show, he defers to the head of the company. You're usually reporting to a network. God help you if you hire that guy or girl that isn't any good. The question comes back, "Where the hell did you find *that*? Where'd you find that terrible girl (or guy)?" You sit there and you say, "I'm never going to do that again! It's gonna be the tried and the true and the safe and the known." How can anybody bum-rap you for hiring Katharine Ross? OK, so she isn't terrific, but she is Katharine Ross. Therefore, you get Katharine Ross. You may meet seven girls who are better than she, but in a very insecure world you begin to play it very safe.

● *So there is a chance you may use a New York actor, even if he has no film on him?*

The possibility of the casting director getting excited about the prospects would be higher. When I first came to Hollywood eleven years ago, I was a New York writer. I didn't know that that was so impressive. They didn't know whether I was a *good* New York writer, but I was a New York writer, and that immediately made me Arthur Miller or Tennessee Williams. For six months I had a whole thing going. Then it wears off. Casting directors are liable to say, "If he did such and such off-Broadway, he must be pretty good, so we'll see him." It doesn't get you the job, but perhaps one step closer to getting in an office.

● *Do you think this applies only to television, or to motion pictures, too?*

I think in movies they tend to gamble a bit more. I would assume they're finding out that Marlon Brando or Robert Redford doesn't guarantee the successful movie. They've also got more time. They can look at a hundred people and screen test them if they want to. On a television show it's impossible; it's a factory. When you have a casting meeting, all the same names come up very quickly. It's the same meeting, week after week after week. If you pass Lois Nettleton the first week and pass her the second week, the third week she'll get the part because now you've run out of Gena Rowlands and Angie Dickinsons. It's the same names; it's musical chairs going from show to show. Yesterday we had to cast a part—a twenty-one-year-old Lauren Bacall. They're not around, because they're not trained. If they're twenty-one and that pretty, you can bet anything they've had no training in the theater. They've probably done two commercials or they were models. They come in, and they're absolutely dismal, and you suffer, and the next thing you start to say is, "Hey, maybe we can make the girl twenty-six." Then you start changing the script and it becomes murder. It's very rare that I find an actor or actress of twenty-one who is trained. There's complete lack of preparation.

If a girl's pretty, somebody says, "Hey, you ought to be an actress." Next thing you know, she's an actress. She goes to some Hollywood workshop for six weeks and gets an agent; God knows how you get an agent. There must be fourteen thousand ways, about thirteen thousand of which are illicit. So she gets an agent, and now she's an actress and being sent on interviews for leads. The producer and director are appalled, because she doesn't even know how to sit in a chair. Before she gets from the door to the chair, you say, "Aw, forget her. She doesn't even know how to walk." There's no training—that's quite clear—and the voices are unbelievable. They're pretty little girls, and they get a couple of roles in "Marcus Welby," and then they disappear. Every year when you look for a young girl, the twenty names submitted are all new. What happened to the other twenty from the year before who were doing the rounds? They're gone. Take Peggy Lipton—five years of making a lot of money in a series . . . never learned word one about acting, never cared to, never took one dramatic lesson in her life, never saw a coach, and was perfectly content with what she was doing.

● *So how did she get the part on "Mod Squad?"*

It was very interesting. First of all, her father was Harold Lipton, a very important man at National General Theatres. Aaron Spelling said, "This might do me some good because some day I might want to make a deal with National General to make a movie." And Peggy was kind of pretty. I'm sure the other girls up for the part weren't much more talented than she, so he said, "Why not? She's got a kind of look, and she'll maybe improve." They didn't really think that show would be a success anyway. That was like Aaron saying, "Well, who can I buy cheapest, 'cause the show stinks anyway."

● *But didn't the viewers love her, and doesn't that mean she was a success?*

Sure. Television's a funny medium. She was a success on that show, in that context. I don't think she'll ever be a success again. She was a kind of personality which the kids obviously reacted to because she was about as vapid as they were. They had the same tastes. There was this empty little blonde running around in dungarees with long hair down to her ass. They didn't care that she couldn't act. I'm fond of Peggy, but I sincerely doubt whether she'll ever get four roles again. Michael Cole never wanted to learn anything. They didn't really care. Clarence Williams at one time wanted to be an actor, but the minute the money started coming in he told me he now had "an image" and there were certain roles he wouldn't play on "Mod Squad" because it would hurt his image with *his* people. Clarence just plain stopped working. He just phoned it in. He once said, "I don't mind being a file cabinet on the show. I'm getting the money." I think I'd go out of my mind with some of the things we gave him to do—standing there, leaning, with the sunglasses, staring at people—but he was happy to do it. He was getting paid five thousand dollars a show. If we were stupid enough to pay him, he was happy enough to take it. He didn't want to be an actor.

I don't know many television stars who want to be actors. I produced "Mod Squad," and I would say that every time we had a show with young people, it was hell on wheels. I remember one incident where there was supposed to be a very swinging, bitchy girl of twenty—a Miss Rich Bitch who's kidnapped and thinks it's a big lark and finds out it isn't. We went through forty girls. That's almost impossible on a television show where you have about four days to cast. It was like a parade, and the poor casting man wasn't terribly good. He just dragged in every young actress in Hollywood and they were all terrible. Eventually, Brenda Scott did the part. Brenda Scott's thirty-one years old. In desperation, we said, "Hey, none of those girls can even say the lines so they make sense." The young people *did not* get the role.

● *When you worked with Burt Reynolds on "Dan August," did he really want to be a serious actor, or was his main objective to be a personality?*

Burt Reynolds was quite honest in saying that he was not a talented actor and that he was an ex-jock football star that had a certain flair for comedy but nobody would ever let him do it. He said, "It's not 'cause I'm really an actor. I can't act, but I can get up smart remarks and can be very charming and very sexy to women. He was furious when we did "Dan August" that we wouldn't let him be sexy and charming to women. We tried to explain to him that a homicide lieutenant, overworked eighteen hours a day and standing in a morgue staring at the body of a fourteen-year-old kid who's been strangled, is not going to make jokes or passes. Burt had a very hard time understanding that. I don't think he really ever thought of himself as an actor, and I don't think he thinks of himself as one today. On the set he would know his lines; he wouldn't fight them, except to complain that he had too many, which is an indication of where somebody's real feelings are. Burt would much rather run and jump over cars, draw guns, shoot, and run into burning buildings, and do all those numbers. He didn't want to act. If he had a difficult scene, he'd say, "Why don't you let so-and-so do it?"

● *So you feel basically that in television a personality is more important than a good actor?*

Absolutely. Good actors are lost. There's nothing for them to act anyway. I would say that on the ten television shows that I've worked on, there wasn't a part that someone could really act and certainly not for a continuing lead. They're all cardboard. "Columbo" is a character because he wears an old raincoat and chews a cigar. End of character. David Janssen as "The Fugitive" was a character because he was on the run. "Cannon" is a character because he's fat. That's character! They're interchangeable. They bought Efrem Zimbalist's personality because Mid-America

liked that fellow. "He's a nice fellow. We trust him." It
has nothing to do with acting; in fact, acting can be a
detriment. If an actor really starts to do something, the
audience gets uncomfortable. Chad Everett, for
example—Chad is a nice fellow, an imitation Clark
Gable. I think that if he tried to do anything, the
viewers wouldn't like it. That guy up there on the tube
is the same fellow they know every week. He's got the
voice; he wears his hair that way; they're comfortable
with him. Why act? I haven't met ten *actors* who've
made it in television. Most of them go down the drain.

● *What about Peter Falk, who really is a good actor? How do
you think he feels when he just walks through a part like
Columbo?*

I think they're relieved that they're finally getting all
the money in the world, and then they get arrogant.
Now, I'm not talking about Peter, because I don't know
him. But usually they change. They become impossible
to live with, because they say, "All those years when I
was good at my craft, right? Nobody would listen and
Quinn Martin said I couldn't act, right? Blah, blah,
blah. And I was ugly. Well, now I want a dressing room
and. . . ." They're monsters! With very rare exceptions
they become monsters.

Last year I had Doug McClure and Tony
Franciosa. Tony's a monster, and I can understand it. I
understand the brutality of working at Universal.
Universal throws Tony into a psychotic state. They
destroyed him as a human being. Now he's a star again,
right? They become impossible with their demands.
They are very angry children, and I haven't met too
many who weren't that way. Bobby Vaughn and David
McCallum were not like that when I produced "Man
from UNCLE." I don't think they thought they were

that big a success, and Bobby wasn't that interested in acting really. It was just a way of making a lot of money. They just happened to be nice guys, but I'd say that most of them are monsters. And if they didn't start out that way, they became it very shortly. With success, terrible things happen to actors. I don't necessarily see it happening to writers, producers, or directors, but with actors, yes.

● *Maybe that's because they've been put down so much all their lives.*

So? Writers are put down even more than actors. But when a Raymond Burr knows that if he walks off the set the studio loses three million dollars on that day, that's a tremendous amount of power and few people can deal with it. I must say I saw Quinn Martin deal with it on two occasions. He fired Bob Lansing at the end of one year on "Twelve O'clock High," and when Paul Burke walked in—he'd been Lansing's replacement—and demanded the production manager be fired for some obscure reason, Quinn said, "You really feel that way, it's you or him?" and Burke said, "You're damn right!" Quinn picked up the phone and said, "Get me Darren McGavin's agent," which ended that rebellion in about two seconds. But there are few guys with as much power and money as Quinn. He's not going to take that shit. Studios like Universal go into shock; they crawl like Pavlov's dog the minute an actor who's in a successful series says he's not coming to work. They go crazy, and that man, that star, *he* runs the show. He fires the producer; he hires the director; he doesn't want to work with that actor; or he just doesn't want to work, because he wants to get a sun bath, and the studio puts up with it. Then, of course, the show goes tremendously over budget. They won't pay the writers or the directors what they deserve, and on top of this they make the secretaries pay for parking! Everybody else gets hurt.

● *Is it possible that the lead in a series would have his nose put out of joint if an "actor" came on and made him work a little harder?*

They get very jealous frequently and quite angry when the other part is better than theirs. I had that constant problem with Tony Franciosa on "Search." If the antagonist was more interesting than he was—which was not too hard, in all fairness to Tony, it's not hard— so here's this other guy who's a bigger-than-life villain, he's got five mistresses, killed fourteen people, and he's a gourmet. Well, Tony would get very uptight and wouldn't want to do that particular show. He would go through it under great strain. We had one show where Dane Clark as a character was more interesting because Dane's wife had been murdered; it was *his* daughter that was in trouble; *he* was wounded and was violating all orders by going on the case. Well, Franciosa got so uptight he kept fluffing Dane Clark's scenes and getting tighter and tighter and tighter. Finally he decided to show that he was better than Dane Clark by doing a stunt that he shouldn't have. He was now going to prove his manhood. So he did the stunt, broke a vertebra in his neck, and was laid up for two weeks. And all because he was paranoid that Dane Clark was coming off better in the show.

● *On the shows you've produced, have you had to be careful that an actor hasn't been taller or better-looking than the star?*

Yes. For instance, on "The FBI" we never cast anybody taller than about five-nine—that's about how tall Efrem Zimbalist is. We hired a new sidekick named Jeff Gould to replace Bill Reynolds, and one of the big things Jeff has going for him is that he slumps. It's a very big thing. It put him half a length in front of any other actor because Efrem doesn't like to play with people who are taller than he is. It's the Alan Ladd syndrome. He doesn't like tall ladies, either.

● *From what you've said up to this point, one gets the feeling that you believe an actor should just learn how to walk and talk and be himself and have a personality that can impress when he walks into an office.*

. . . And have a competent agent. Don't embarrass anybody. I've seen good actors actually embarrass executive producers just because they were actors. I've seen executives get very uncomfortable and say, "What are they doing?" For example, I saw Joan Hackett drive an executive producer right up the wall because she was doing something interesting with the role. He didn't want anything done with it; he wanted her to say the words. "She's a murder suspect. Let her just be a murder suspect. Why is she doing all those other things? Sure, they may be interesting, but I don't want them. I want the audience to be interested in the part, not her."

● *Then, to a great extent, you also feel it's purely the gimmick in television? David Carradine in "Kung Fu"?*

Yeah, it's the gimmick and also the time slot. To prove a point, when I did "Dan August" it was not a successful series. I don't think we ever got more than a twenty-seven share.* We were well reviewed; people thought the show was good, but it didn't make it. Now CBS Network has it on prime time, and it's a big hit.

● *Isn't that because Burt Reynolds is a big star now?*

It could be, or it could just be that we had a deadly time spot when we originally came on. They put us against

---

*This refers to the industry poll indicating degree of audience viewing.

two established detective shows. We were on the weakest of the three networks and with no promotion. Now, how are you gonna make it with all that going for you? They threw us against "Hawaii Five-O," which was in the top ten, and a tremendous trilogy coming out of Universal with tremendous publicity, and there we were on little ABC with no promotion, no publicity, plus nobody knew Burt Reynolds from a hole in the wall. Now it's a big hit. I understand that overnight it's in the top ten. CBS is going crazy. If Quinn Martin will only do it with Burt Reynolds they'll give us eight hour-and-a-halfs firm. Quinn says, "I can deliver Darren McGavin; I can deliver Leslie Nielsen; but I can't deliver Burt Reynolds anymore." Now ABC is saying, "We pulled the trigger on that show too fast." Yes, they did pull it too fast; that's obvious, quite obvious.

● *So what about all those years of hard and dedicated study that some actors go through?*

That's only if you love acting. It's not going to do a damn thing for your career. Geraldine Page did not become a movie star; neither did Eli Wallach. And now you're talking about brilliant actors. For television and most film—unless you're very beautiful, unless when you walk in an office and six heads come up because you're that good-looking—yeah, I think it's bullshit.

● *So then if you're that good-looking you think you don't need to have the training?*

Not exactly. Being that good-looking will get you in the door and might get you a part, but if you're embarrassing on the screen. . . . So you have to study a little, enough so you're not embarrassing.

● *Does anyone ever say, "Let's find a couple of new actors and really make stars out of them"?*

No. What they say is, "Let's find a couple of safe actors and don't bother me with making stars." They're not star-makers.

● *When you produced "Mod Squad" for Aaron Spelling, weren't all of those kids new, unknown actors?*

They were new but also cheap. They were very cheap, and I don't think anybody had much conviction about the show. You can't find established actors at nineteen anyway—much less three of them—so they took a chance on three unknown kids. Tige Andrews I'm sure was hired because he was cheap. But now those kids are finished. They're like rock-and-roll stars—two years, three years, and then, "Goodbye and good luck"— because they never learned anything about their craft. Also, a lot of big television stars fail the second time out. Sometimes it's because of the show. David Janssen has failed three times now since "The Fugitive." Movie stars fail in television, also, because there's a basic misconception at the network that if you get a star, you have a hit. Jimmy Garner proved that wasn't true, and so did Rod Taylor.

● *Well, could it be that once the public has accepted David Janssen as the character in "The Fugitive" it may be hard for them to adjust to seeing him as another character in another show?*

Well, Raymond Burr went from thirteen years as Perry Mason into "Ironside."

● *Yes, but that was so close to what he'd already been playing in "Perry Mason." I'm sure a lot of people wouldn't have known the difference between the character in the two shows.*

Except that now he's sitting in a wheelchair! That's about the depth of characterizations you get on television. Does he stand or does he sit? Is he fat or is he thin? It's hysterical when you sell a television series and you write a background on the star: where he came from, what school he went to, how many times he's been married, his war record, why he got into this. It's never on the screen. And you keep writing presentations and you read them and say, "What the hell, this will never be on the screen. What it will be is this man chasing another man in a car."

● *If you were to come to Hollywood as an actor, what would be the first thing you'd do?*

I'd have plastic surgery and make sure I was damn good-looking to start off with. Fred Silverman, the vice president at CBS, said he wouldn't buy a Dennis Hopper for television if his life depended on it, and he's telling the truth, because for every Peter Falk that makes it, there are nineteen pretty boys that still make it. Bill Conrad's a rare exception. Certainly girls have to be pretty. I can't think of four ugly girls who are big in television. I guess you could say Carol Burnett isn't too pretty, but then she's a comedienne. I can't think of many who lasted long. The girl who did *Diary of a Mad Housewife,* Carrie Snodgrass—she's now being offered around to television shows, but what are you going to do with her? She's a good actress, but most fellows when they go to a movie want to see a pretty girl. I saw Jeannie Berlin in *Heartbreak Kid* and I wouldn't ever want to see her again in my life. A girl in this town has a hell of a lot better chance if she's really exciting to look at. She may be a great actress if she's ugly, and the director may say, "Isn't she wonderful," but the audience says, "Who cares!" People still want a certain amount of romance, even if it's Mamie Van Doren. If you're a truckdriver, that's what you want. If a girl wants to be an actress, assuming she's crazy enough to want to do it, she'd better be damn good-looking and be prepared to work damn hard.

● *So a pretty girl comes to Los Angeles and joins Actors Studio or a so-called reputable workshop. What then?*

Get some publicity! Get known! I remember Roddy McDowall, years ago when we were doing "Matinee Theatre" and his career wasn't going too well. There was an actor who'd just been busted for attempted rape and he made big headlines. Roddy said, "Now I know what I've been doing wrong."

● *Do you think the* Cosmopolitan *centerfold helped Burt Reynolds become the star he is today?*

Absolutely! If you're a political candidate or an actor, you must have exposure. Being honest, I'll be sitting in my office and the casting lady will say to me, "Well, what about JoAnn Harris?" I stop for a second. I don't know who JoAnn Harris is from the rear of a tank. Why should I? Then I remember that a director who had worked for me said, "There's a terrific little actress, JoAnn Harris. Boy, I'd like to screw her." That was the quote, I remember it. So I said, "Why don't you bring her in." Only because somebody had said something about her and I remembered it. She happened to be very good, and she got the part. But if somebody hadn't said, "Hey, she's a great-looking girl and, boy, would I like to screw her"— even that's exposure. Otherwise it's just a name, JoAnn Harris. What do I want to meet a JoAnn Harris for? It's terribly important that we recognize a name.

● *Do you think it will change? What about the sex films?*

No, it won't change. You'll get three years of pornography, which will practically wipe out Hollywood as we know it, and then after that when the fourteen-year-old

American public gets tired of watching people screw, maybe it'll become a business. But the first three years will be a disaster.

● *Do you think it hurts an actor to do pornography?*

It murders them. Who wants to touch them after that? Because at some point when they become identified with having done it, there's still a very square America out there, and they don't like it.

● *What about "Movies of the Week"?\* Do you think there's more opportunity there?*

No; less, because the networks want to approve every member of the cast. When I was doing a pilot which would have been a "Movie of the Week" for NBC and Metromedia last year, I had to submit a cast list of the people I was thinking about—not that I was *hiring*, but who I was thinking about hiring. I had Al Tresconi, a casting man, sitting over at NBC crossing off the people that NBC didn't like. There were not too many left on the list!

They have this thing called TV Q. It's in my office—a big, thick thing that has every actor from A to Z listed in it and also audience acceptance of each actor. It's a whole thing. And then the actor gets a final mark: well known, very well known, partially known, not well known. Are they well liked, not liked—it's like a Gallup Poll. You can go to the actor's score: 140, 130, 120. You'd be surprised to find that Richard Burton's practically at the bottom and Tige Andrews is practically at the top, and the network, between those two people, would take Tige Andrews. It's as simple as that. That's how you do a pilot. It has nothing to do

*Films made for television.

with talent. The network says, "Look, Stu Whitman's got a 53. Hey, wait a minute, Andy Duggan's got a 54. We'll take Andy Duggan." It doesn't matter whether he's right for the role. It's the computer.

You try and do a pilot, and you go out of your mind. If you look at "Movies of the Week" you see the same people on it all the time. Lloyd Bridges does ten a year; Darren McGavin does eight or so. They're well recognized names to the public, and why are they recognized? Because they do all the "Movies of the Week"! It's a vicious circle. And that's how the network will sit on a pilot. It's got nothing to do with whether they think the guy's a good actor. First of all, they have no way of knowing. They're soap salesmen!

● *Do you believe that a pretty well-known star of film is wise to take a television series?*

Television has made stars, but stars haven't made television. All the big movie stars that came into television—maybe one or two made it, but most of the people who became stars on television were not known before, in any other medium. I think that's a lesson that's been forgotten by networks, who become more fearful each year instead of more brave. "We gotta get a name; we gotta get a name!" That's all you hear. Ten years ago they didn't have to get a name, and television made stars. Mary Tyler Moore, Dick Van Dyke—these people were made by television. Who were they before? But that they've forgotten.

Now, I'm trying to do a pilot, and they're driving me up the wall with incredible requests. "Do you think you can get Bobby Redford?" I said, jokingly, "Well, I don't know about Redford, but I can guarantee Paul Newman." Their answer? "Well, he's a little older. We think Redford would be better." I said, "Paul's gonna be terribly hurt when I tell him." And they looked at me, finally beginning to get the idea that I was kidding. They said, "You don't think they'll do it? We can give them forty or fifty thousand dollars a show." I said, "No; they're not ready for it." One guy popped up and said, "Well, I don't want them anyway. Look what Jimmy Garner did to us last year." I said, "Well, so much for Newman and Redford! We will now move on to somebody else." And their question? "How about Cameron Mitchell?" I nearly fell off the back of the chair. I like Cameron; he's a nice guy. But how the hell did we go from Redford and Newman to Cameron Mitchell? And those are the meetings you have. They're real exercises in insanity.

● *How do these people get into those executive positions at the networks?*

They certainly don't come up through show business. They come up from selling time, from being salesmen for the networks or working on local stations. They're so-called bright, charming, and wear the right clothes, and as there are a lot of firings they move up the ladder. They become one of the "in" group, and then one day you're looking at a guy who is the vice president and who has never made one foot of film in his life—doesn't know anything about the business—and he's sitting and saying, "Well, I don't like him." That's what you live with. Some of them are nice people; some of them are just pains in the ass, but none of them has ever done a show. Last year I was in a meeting with the guy who was in charge of program development at one of the networks. How he got that job I don't know, because he was a young kid, his sexuality I wouldn't swear to, and he knew absolutely nothing. I was in talking about a new television series, and after about two minutes I realized this kid knew nothing about what a television series was and how you made one—knew absolutely nothing. There he is sitting behind this enormous desk, pontificating, and I said to myself, "Hey, Tony, control your temper," because my inclination was to say, "Hey, why don't you go fuck yourself," and leave. But I'm there with a studio executive, so I'm polite. When we walk out, the studio executive says to me, "He's an idiot." I replied, "He's not an idiot; he's a moron." Flash forward: Nine months later the network kicked him out on his behind because they had a disastrous program development. Do you know where he is now? At that studio, in charge of all two-hour movies made for television. That's par for the course, and it was a studio executive who said to me, "He's an idiot," but *his* studio hired him. Why? It's simple. Because they think he's got contacts within the network. They're not hiring him because they think he's got talent or knows how to make movies. They hire him because, maybe, he's "in" with the higher-ups at the network, and that way they'll get more two-hour movies for television through his contacts. Case after case after case is exactly that. It's a club, but the club is not based on any particular knowledge. They don't last long, these chaps, but they do get their shot. They're there for three years or so and then disappear into some great beyond, and that's how it happens.

# Walter Matthau

## Actor

"People are always afraid of extremely talented people . . . .
They try to squash them."

Walter Matthau was born in New York on October 1, 1923, and graduated from Seward Park High School, where he won letters in basketball, track, handball, and ping-pong. He served in the air force for four years during World War II, and when he returned to New York, it was to study journalism at Columbia University. But after a summer of acting with a stock company in Erie, Pennsylvania, he knew what he wanted to do. He has since received an Oscar for his film portrayal of the lawyer in *The Fortune Cookie* and a pair of Tony Awards for his Broadway roles in *A Shot in the Dark* and *The Odd Couple.*

Films

*A Face in the Crowd*
*The Kentuckian*
*Slaughter on Tenth Avenue*
*Indian Fighter*
*No Power on Earth*
*Middle of the Street*
*Onion Head*
*Voice in the Mirror*
*King Creole*
*Lonely Are the Brave*
*Strangers When We Meet*
*Who's Got the Action?*
*The Gangster Story (also
    written and directed
    by Matthau)*
*Charade*
*Goodbye Charlie*

*Mirage*
*The Fortune Cookie*
*A Guide for the
    Married Man*
*The Odd Couple*
*Candy*
*Hello, Dolly!*
*Cactus Flower*
*A New Leaf*
*Plaza Suite*
*Kotch*
*Pete 'N' Tillie*
*Charley Varrick*
*Pelham 1-2-3*
*The Front Page*
*The Sunshine Boys*

We met with Walter for lunch at the Beverly Hills Tennis Club. He always eats there, outside, beside the pool. His first question to us was, "Is either of you for Nixon?" With our negative response, we were hugged, wined and dined, and given the following interview. Walter Matthau is terribly appealing—droll, witty, amusing, never missing a trick. We got along fine—on politics and on love of the theater and onions!

- *When did you suddenly become successful?*

    Well, "suddenly" is a misnomer. It happened over twenty years and it happened with a two-punch posture. A two-punch posture is a left and right that knocks out your opponent. My left was *A Shot in the Dark,* and my right was *The Odd Couple,* and that was it. That was the one-two shot that said, "Oh, this guy can be funny; he's a comedian as well as an actor. And he can now be even more valuable to us because he can make people laugh and people want to laugh. They identify with him and will go to see him."

- *Today the young actors all seem to look alike—no energy, no individuality. Why are there no Clark Gables and Carole Lombards today?*

    Well, someone started a new school of acting—no energy. With all the amplification that you have today, that seems to be the form of acting that is most acceptable as being realistic. If you speak clearly, you're a phony. But that'll change. It's in the process of changing back to where they're using people who have some kind of talent, either external or internal.

- *Do you believe a young actor should knock himself out studying when the requirements in television and even some films are so low?*

    I think it's very good for the person to have a stage background, because that's the basic metal in acting. You're out there; you can't be camouflaged with a tricky director. If you do have this skill, this stage experience, you can go from there and you can do whatever you want. It's much easier, because that's the basic metal of it. But you can become a star without learning how to act at all on the stage. There are many stars of television and movies who you can't hear past the second row and who wash out and who are totally boring and uninteresting on the stage, and yet they're big stars in movies and television. Amplification again. Close-ups.

● *But if you were to start out today as an actor, what would be the steps you'd take?*

I would try to get into a play. I think a play is the thing that will sharpen your basic foundation so that you can walk in and say, "Well, I'm an actor. How do I know I'm an actor? Well, I've done some plays. I've been on the stage. I've said lines and acted with people, and there was an audience there and no one said 'cut'; no one tricked me and made splices and so forth. I was acting on a stage."

● *What made you become an actor? Where did you begin?*

I guess it was a lot of things all coming together at the right time and staying in place. I didn't know what else to do. I got out of high school and I went to the CCC camp and then into the service. All during my childhood I'd gravitated toward reciting, toward being in plays. That and sports—playing baseball, soccer, ping-pong, handball—and drama. And then, during World War II, I was in the army and afterward had the opportunity to go to school and get ninety bucks a month as a student. Ninety bucks a month was interesting. Being a student in drama school was interesting, and it gave me something to do that I liked. The school I went to was the Dramatic Workshop of the New School for Social Research. That gave me the opportunity to act on the stage. They had a theater with 299 seats to qualify just under the union scale.

As I was going to school, I was looking around for opportunities to get into a play—any kind of play—and television was just coming into the average citizens' homes. That was 1946. TV wasn't a reality yet. I was looking for work, keeping my eyes open, reading all of the papers and so forth and so on, and getting little jobs here and there on the stage doing all kinds of different plays in settlement houses, in churches, in saloons— wherever they had a stage and wherever they were doing a play. I did anything and everything. They didn't know what to make of me. I was neither a leading man type—which I still am not—nor was I quite a character actor—which I still am not. I was neither fish nor fowl, so it was difficult at first to cast me. Sort of a tall, young, plain-looking actor. What was it about me that made me get a lot of jobs? I was commercially exploitable. I could be a detective, a gangster, a lawyer, or a doctor. I fell into things. Whatever they needed, I could play a gangster very easily, a lawyer, a policeman, and those were the commercially usable types, and so it was that I fell into those jobs and was able to do them competent-ly. I immediately started earning a living at acting.

● *Did you do anything in your career that you felt was wrong?*

No. I knew that a lot of plays I was in weren't going to work, but I would do the same thing if I had to do it over again because I had to work.

● *Did you feel that you would become a star?*

No.

● *What did you feel? What did you want? What was your goal?*

I never thought about it. I wanted to get my ninety

dollars a month from Uncle Sam, go to school and look around, maybe get a date with some girls, and maybe go to a ball game at the Garden, which was nearby. I played every day. I didn't have any long-range plans.

● *Do you enjoy acting?*
Enormously. I still do.

● *Do you feel that you've reached the peak of your career?*
No. I don't think so. I think I became a very successful actor but certainly didn't reach what I thought I could do. Somewhere along the line I thought I was much better than Olivier in Shakespeare and thought perhaps I was handicapped by my American accent. I cursed the day I wasn't born in England so that I could do all those Shakespearean plays. But then, I *did* do a lot of Shakespeare. As a matter of fact, in my first Broadway play I was an old English bishop. That was *Ann of a Thousand Days,* and nobody, including Rex Harrison, knew that I wasn't English. As a matter of fact, Leland Hayward, the producer, came back and said, "Hey, who's the new old Englishman?"

● *Would you ever go back to Broadway and do a play?*
I think about it three or four minutes every six months and then give it up. It's too much work. I don't like to work. I like easy work, and doing movies is easy work.

● *Isn't it part of an actor's training that he learn to work with bad directors?*
Yes, no question about it. You've got to give as well as the director. I've noticed, especially in the last twenty years, the young stars come in and won't give anything. They're all so wrapped up in their own little private part—and I mean that literally—that they just don't care about you or the director or anything else. *They*

*want to feel it themselves.* I think that's a lot of
nonsense.
● *Are you very careful about who the director is on a specific
project before you commit to it?*
    I'm casually careful. I mean if it's a director that I've
worked with before and that I didn't like, I'll say, "No,
thank you," but there are very few of those. I like most
directors.
● *If you had to advise an actor today how to begin, what
would you say is the most important thing he should do?*
    The first thing you do is try and dissuade them, and if
they won't be dissuaded, then you say, "OK, go to New
York, stay in New York, and try to get a job on the stage.
Just go and see everybody who's casting a play and ask
them for a job."
● *Why would you want to dissuade them?*
    There are so few jobs. For every 150 good people, there's
maybe one job, and for every 150 good people, I would
say there are 1,500 people who are incompetent. And
let's say ten percent of 1,500 are competent, and one
person gets the job. That means 149 people who are
competent don't get the job, don't work. That's why I
try to dissuade them. I don't dissuade them with any
passion pleas. I just say, "Now here are the facts. Your
chances of being an actor who makes more than six
hundred dollars a year are about one in five thousand."
That's all.
● *Do you think it's easier if you look like Errol Flynn or if
you're a beautiful girl?*
    It was up until the time things started going well for
me. I looked at Errol Flynn yesterday in something or
other and I thought, "My God, he's pretty." I've never

seen anyone so pretty, except for Madeleine Carroll, and she's a woman.

● *Did you want to be in films when you first started acting?*
No. I pooh-poohed films. I was much too good for films, and I swore up and down that I'd never be in a film. They'd never get me out there to that phony place. I would never sell my soul.

● *Now that you've sold it, how do you feel?*
Wonderful! It's the only place to be.

● *Why is it that some of the young stars rise very quickly and don't sustain? Do you think it has to do with timing—that the audience today is more fickle than a few years back? Is it possible to build your kind of a career anymore? Take, for instance, a Dustin Hoffman?*
Well, it may be that a Dustin Hoffman is just very particular. He may have fewer needs than other people. Some people start to get successful; they buy a big house and a couple of cars, a yacht; they maintain certain standards that they've suddenly thrust themselves into. A Dustin Hoffman may require fifty dollars a month, so he can be very choosy about his art. I do a lot of crap. For example, in Europe a man or a woman becomes a star and is a star until he or she dies. Here, you have to prove yourself every picture. In Europe you have a background, and it's not all dependent upon a smash-hit performance and enormous box-office receipts, and so you last longer.

● *Do you think that a person can do too much?*
Yes, I think so. Especially if you're a high-level, box-office-spectacular, smash-hit-type actor. Then you've got to choose very carefully. In England if a man's just a fine actor, he can work all the time and not worry about his salary or his box-office rating.

● *In choosing your roles, do you think in terms of what the public wants to see you do?*

No. I do what I want to do until I run out of money, which is about every six months, and then I do whatever comes around.

● *Jack Lemmon said he gets so involved in a role that he literally becomes that character and has difficulty after working hours divorcing himself from the part. Do you find it much easier?*

Yes, I find it easy to divorce myself from the role I'm playing as far as I know. But my wife, Carol, will say, "Just a minute, I think you're still in character."

● *Is the script the basis for your electing to do a film, or are there other elements such as who's going to play opposite you, who's the director, and so on?*

Primarily it's the script. But you can take a good script and give it a lousy director and the picture gets murdered. Or you can take a so-so script, get a great director . . . I just did a picture called *Charley Varrick*, the biggest pile of horseshit you ever saw in your life. It was so bad that I wanted to do it. But I liked the director, Don Siegel, a funny man, a delightful man, and it actually looks like a movie!

● *Does it help to know the actors you're working with before you go into a scene?*

And how! I used to start arguments in films when I'd fly in from New York to do a film. I'd get on the set and I'd start arguing with the director about the script or whatever. I feel that if you have an argument with someone, you're immediately on better terms with him later, after you resolve it. So you have some social contact with him. I see a lot of films. I look and I say, "Those people don't know each other. They don't know what the hell they're talking about. They don't know who they are or where they're going or what they're doing."

● *Have you always had an agent?*

Yes. I changed agents every three months. As soon as they got used to me and my salary. When they begin to say, "Well, you're a three-hundred-dollar-a-day actor," and I say "No, three hundred thousand dollars," and they say, "Now come on, don't kid me; I know you're a three-hundred-dollar-a-day actor," I say, "Goodbye." I don't have the slightest loyalty for an agent. My agent is flawless in his bad taste. If he likes something, I know I'm not going to do it.

● *Do you find that scripts submitted to you all tend to be for the same kind of Walter Matthau part?*

Well, if they say it's a Walter Matthau part, the chances of my reading it are slim, because I know it's not a Walter Matthau part—it's a Lou Blau part. He's my lawyer.

● *Are you with a large agency?*

Yes, I happened to be with a large agency when the big money started coming in, so I stayed with them. They're totally useless, and they make a fortune.

● *Would you suggest that a young actor go with a smaller agent until he "makes it"?*

Probably. Usually the agent doesn't do any work; the agent's a promoter, a hustler. He's not pushing anybody.

● *Going back to your own experience, was going on interviews ever a problem for you?*

In order to be a good actor you unfortunately must have a large vulnerable area—an extraordinarily sensitive area—and in order to be a successful actor, you must do away with that large vulnerable and sensitive area. You must stow it. There's the conflict. If you successfully blunt your vulnerability, you're less of an actor but you have more of a chance for success. If the actor goes on an interview, then he's already lost some of his vulnerability, and in order to get a job you've got to go on an interview. Ok. You'll never hear that put more brilliantly. I don't care who you speak to!

● *Do you think a person can be too good today?*

Yes. People are always afraid of extremely talented people. They always are. They try to squash them when they're younger. As they get older, then they can assert themselves. Whatever they're talented in begins to seep through, and then they're respected. Mediocrity is easier to cope with in the beginning, but mediocrity won't last very long.

● *Did you ever have any trouble trying to convince a producer that you could play a certain part?*

All the time. Even today. Sometimes I'm wrong, and sometimes the agents are wrong. They can try to oversell you. An agent was trying to sell Connie Towers to Abe Burrows recently. Abe Burrows said, "Connie Towers! She's much too tall for the role," and the agent said, "Have you seen her lately?"

● *Having worked with some of the best actors in the film business, such as Cary Grant, Audrey Hepburn, and so on, what is your opinion of the up-and-coming young actors?*

Unprofessional for the most part. They subscribe to the theory that one must *feel it*, and I think that kind of acting belongs on the psychoanalyst's couch. I don't care whether *you* feel it; the *audience* has to feel it. You've had some soda and a large salad, and you've got to do Lady Macbeth or Ophelia and you don't feel like doing it. It's a rainy Tuesday night. You don't feel it. Yeah, but there are eight hundred people out there who paid five or ten dollars apiece, and you've got to get out there and do it. But the young actor today, what does he need a job for? Somebody's gonna feed him. So he doesn't really need a job. He doesn't have to be an actor either, probably isn't.

● *Do you prefer Hollywood to New York?*

There's too much sunshine here, and I don't think your brain can operate as well. With all due respect, I think in a colder climate your brain works better. I think that when you come out here you're really in a state of semiretirement. It's just too paradisiacal.

● *Is it important for an actor to be aware of life?*

Yeah. I think that's why there were better actors thirty years ago. You had to go out and work in order to stay alive. Today you don't, and anyway, I'm in a different circle of people now. I know mostly rich people, and their children don't have to work. Their children don't know anything. They don't have to reach out. They don't have to struggle. They don't grow. So, although the children are in a sense more knowledgeable about certain things because they've sat in front of a television set for thirty years, they don't know anything about what life is. But then I also begin to think: Why is life more real if you have to' struggle and you have to join the CCC camps and you have to get on a ship—get on a tanker and stoke coal? Why is that more real than just sitting in a nice, two-hundred-dollar-a-month apartment?

● *Do you think you'll ever do any television?*

Oh, yes. I probably will be a has-been in a couple of years and I'll start doing television. It's a graveyard for old actors and aspiring young actors.

# Albert S. Ruddy
## Producer

"But the scary thing about this business is that you may make the biggest commitment in the world and end up busted."

Albert S. Ruddy was born in Montreal, Canada, but moved to New York City at the age of seven. He attended Brooklyn Tech, a high school for gifted children, and earned a scholarship to City College of New York, where he majored in chemical engineering. After two years he changed his mind and decided on something more creative. He graduated from the School of Architecture at the University of Southern California. After many side trips into other fields, such as a stint at the Rand Corporation, Al Ruddy decided to concentrate on Hollywood. He created the successful TV series "Hogan's Heroes" and produced the following feature films:

*The Wild Seed*
*Little Fauss and Big Halsey*
*The Godfather*
*The Longest Yard*

Al Ruddy, the producer of *The Godfather,* is a ruggedly handsome, amusing man in his early forties. We met with him in his sumptuously decorated offices at Paramount Studios. As you walk down the corridor toward his suite, your eye cannot help but notice the large gold lettering *ASR* covering the whole of the entrance door. Ridding himself of his long-haired, blue-jeaned coterie, Al Ruddy ushered us into his private, grandiose office. As he sat, his bare feet on the desk, he nibbled on vitamin C pills when he wasn't chewing gum or smoking cigars. He gave us a thoroughly detailed account of the building of his "empire" and told how, as a smart businessman, his eye always turned toward the dollar and how he made it to the top.

Albert S. Ruddy

● *What would you tell the young student or graduate who wants to make a career in this business?*

That you're really gambling in this business with the two most valuable things you have: your time and your youth. We can only tell a kid so many things. With a mother-son relationship, or father-son relationship, you can know all the right answers and try and tell your kid what he should or should not do, but it's very difficult. When I came into this business, I had been an architect and had thought of myself as a very creative person. But you have to learn what it's all about, so I guess only *you* can figure it out, which is why I say the quicker you get out there the more rapidly you will get to the point of either committing to stay in or *really* getting out.

I know a guy—he was a very fine actor and he never made a living acting. The guy's forty years old now and he's selling life insurance at Seal Beach. If he had got into selling life insurance when he was twenty-five he'd be president of the company today. You're not going to get the job as trainee at DuPont when you're thirty-five. Forget it; it's too late. Those jobs are for guys that are graduating from college *this* year, this September. So what you've got to do is maximize your time.

● *Do you believe that the acting profession is more of a "business" than most people think it is? And do you think there is a formula for success?*

I find in retrospect, looking back, that there is not that much correlation between talent and success in this business. Very few people can take the gaff and the emotional frustration of this business, and the ones who hang in there—the women—are the people who are so overwhelmed with the need for this business they're willing to sacrifice everything—all the practical considerations, the emotional abuse, all the things that most people need to maintain the semblance of normalcy. They'll give it all up to *make it.*

Somebody should start to make these young people aware of the other aspect of this business and, in a sense, the most important aspect. I mean, you've got to be ready to have that door slammed in your face. Those kids out there don't have the faintest idea of the business of show business. They sit there and watch Eisenstein and Truffaut, and they look at all the great filmmakers. Believe me, to graduate from college today, no matter how much talent and ability you may bring with you, it's like being alone in the Grand Canyon and seeing what you want on the south rim and you're on the north rim. That's how far it is, and they haven't the faintest idea how to do it. They walk up and say, "Well, here I am!" and they get punched in the face, run over, and left behind.

● *As producer of one of the greatest financial and artistic motion picture successes,* The Godfather, *could you tell us how you got into this business and what your background was?*

I worked as an architect. I worked as a computer specialist, an assistant developer in land, and I always kept vacillating, never really devoting twenty-four hours a day to thinking about this business. And then Eliot Kastner told me one day, "Look, if you want to be in this business, you've got to forget everything else. You've got to stop thinking even in your mind that if it doesn't work out you can go back to designing. The minute you get to that point you'll be on the road to making it. It must be a total, *total* commitment."

But my theory is, if you decide to make that total commitment, I would like to think more futures might be saved if you could find out within a fairly sane period of time—if you think you can make it, if you think you can't make it, if you want to stay in. I mean, shit, I would rather do it in two years than fifteen. I'm not saying you can't say in two years, "Well, I may not make it, but I like it, so I'm willing to struggle and live like this." That's cool, but you may say, "No, I can't take it—the struggle, the abuse—and so I'm getting out."

● *What is the big difference between this business and any other business?*

The reality of the business is such that, if you study to become a doctor, there's no way you're going to starve. You can study to become an actor and starve for the rest of your life. There's a very big difference in spite of the fact that they're both true professions, and in a sense acting takes, in my opinion, even more talent than medicine generally. But as we all know, there are many talented actors who never had enough money to buy a good meal, so your existence in the framework of this society becomes your ultimate choice. And if you're not going to make a living as an actor or even as a director, then you have to answer the basic question in your life: "Is trying to get even one television show more important to me than ever owning a house, than ever owning a car, or being able to go to Europe?" If you can evaluate it on that level, it's fantastic. But the scary thing about this business is that you may make the biggest commitment in the world and end up busted. No one guarantees you. If you go to medical school, you can almost be guaranteed seventy-five thousand dollars a year when you get out because that's what most doctors make—and not great doctors. You don't find that in show business. If there are one thousand kids studying acting today and if ten of those kids are working five years from now, that's a very high percentage.

● *Do you believe, then, that an actor, or anybody in this business, should put a limit on the time he will spend trying to make it?*

I don't think you can put a time limit on it. By that I mean you can't say a year, two years. It's too variable from person to person. But I *do* think we know at the bottom ultimately what the truth is. I then think you have to have the courage when you reach that point to accept the reality of the business and say, "I want it, but I can't make it, so I'm going to go and do something else." A lot of people get lazy; they get used to the life style of sitting around the house; they go to Schwab's; and they like the idea of saying they're an actor. That's a very hard mold to break. But I do think everyone, and I mean everyone, reaches a flash point. It may be corny to say "a moment of truth," but it's true. There *is* a time if you're bright enough and perceptive enough and honest enough with yourself when you know you're not going to make it, and I think that's the point when you just have to pick up the marbles and go.

● *When preparing a film, what importance do you yourself place on the casting? Is the star the most vital element for financial success?*

The realities of this business today are that there are very few really big names, as there were ten years ago. Outside of Clint Eastwood, maybe, nobody guarantees you your money. But let's say that we're dealing with ten major stars. Generally your production is centered around one or two of these major stars. Once you get past Robert Redford, Paul Newman, or Burt Reynolds, the minute you cast the top you can use unknowns in all the other parts. I find it's almost bizarre that there's more opportunity today in motion pictures than there is in television—for anything major, that is. You may get one shot in a "Marcus Welby," but when they're going to cast pilots today the networks have their list of acceptable actors, and they won't hire an actor to do a lead in a pilot if he's not on the network's list. Whereas in motion pictures, if you have Burt Reynolds or Clint Eastwood, you have fifteen other parts to cast with whoever you want.

● *Do you believe that the film today has taken over where the star used to be—that the film itself is the box-office draw?*

No question about it. Any two people talking about movies ten years ago, one guy would say, "Gee, I saw a great movie," and the other would say, "Who was in it?" Today when someone says, "Gee, I saw a great movie," the other says, "What's it about?" That's it. You see, people are too sophisticated today, and I don't mean in the intellectual sense. They've been so inundated with television and communication that they don't want to see Paul Newman in a bad movie; it doesn't matter to them.

● *Maybe the public has become more fickle in recent years in the sense that they really don't want to see too much of any one particular "star." Maybe they'd prefer to see an unknown sometimes.*

My feeling is . . . I would put it this way, and we're now talking about dollars and cents, right? In my opinion, the ideal film to make is a great film with major stars like *Butch Cassidy and the Sundance Kid*— a perfect example. A great piece of material and two major stars. Ideally, that's the way I'd prefer to go.

● *What about* The Godfather—*did you feel you had that kind of situation with that film?*

You have to remember that the star of *The Godfather* was the book, and the writer Mario Puzo. The book was on the best-seller list for a year and a half before we made the film, and we had the finest English speaking actor in the world, Marlon Brando. Brando was not really a bankable star at that point and, because of that, there was a great reluctance on Paramount's part to go with Brando. We had a big fight, because under no conditions did they want Brando.

● *Who did they want?*

They didn't have any particular idea. The godfather was the first part we cast because it was pivotal on building the architecture of the film. But they said, "Marlon Brando! Brando does not only *not* bring people in; he keeps people out." That was not only Paramount's feeling but the consensus of people in Film Financing. Paramount was the only studio that finally bought Brando. You could never have sold him at Columbia or Universal.

● *What finally changed their minds?*

Screen tests. We tested most of the actors we thought could be strong possibilities. They were not conventional screen tests. We had a little Sony videotape machine, and instead of keeping photos we had them put on tape, and we now have permanent three-dimensional records with sound of these people.

● *In respect to the future of the film industry, about fifteen years or so ago the big studios used to find actors they thought had possibilities, put them under contract, and build stars. How does an actor build his career today? Is it hit-or-miss and that's it?*

There is no studio anymore which is involved in that

kind of operation outside of a television operation like Universal, and if you look at the records that the studios have over the last ten or fifteen years, it's pathetic. The reason you can't build stars is you must have continued and extended production to be able to finance the development of a star. For me to put somebody under contract for three or four hundred dollars per week, for openers, that costs me twenty thousand dollars—right? Including fringe benefits, maybe thirty or forty thousand dollars. That means you are now in the business of trying to find movies for your contract players. I'm doing a film that starts in Oklahoma, a prison story, so if I had a girl under contract I sure as hell can't put her in it, so I'm carrying thirty or forty thousand dollars' fee in the hopes of getting her in another picture. You should never seriously compromise the quality of your film by forcing somebody you have under contract into the part.

● *So what does the actor do today? Obviously, he can't rely on someone to take him by the hand, put him under contract, and pay him X number of dollars a week.*

Today you try to get into television, where a lot of actors are working. Jess Oppenheimer, who produced the "I Love Lucy" show, said, "Let me tell you something, Al. The hardest thing to make in the motion picture business is a living, and the easiest thing to make is money!" It happens to be very true. If you're worried about paying your rent, you may as well get out. He also said, "I can't tell you or anyone else how to get into this business or how to make it in this business, but the only thing I know is the people that want it—who really want it and need it—somehow gravitate to the top." And I think that's very true. If I were an actor, I'd be living in Hollywood and in order to keep moving my

career ahead I would do at least one thing every day—
one thing—I don't care if it's seeing an agent, a casting
director, a producer, a director, a writer. It's got to be
done because you never know when the opportunity's
going to come.

● *When you're casting a picture and you want to use an*
*unknown, does the studio give you much static?*

Well, you must realize that we're an independent
company, and generally when I take a piece of material
to a studio, the leads are cast and, naturally, you share
the same concern for the ultimate success of the film as
the finance people. We all want the same thing; we
want to make a film that will not only be good but will
return its investment and hopefully a profit. Otherwise
we won't have a business left. So you cannot close out
communication with studio people. It's a much smaller
group, and we have much closer contact with each
other. We know each other's needs. We also have much
more sympathetic feelings to each other's problems,
because at certain moments the business gets pretty
ragged on the edge.

We had a big fight about Brando, right? We got
Brando. It takes a certain finesse, and it takes
appreciating the other person's position. What happens is you get into a room and you say, "Ok, now let's
talk the fucking thing out." And you tell them why you
want him, and they tell you why they don't, and
ultimately because you're right you will prevail. I have
very rarely seen a complete deadlock so completely
pulverized to the point that people walked out because
they couldn't resolve the problem. Most studios are
going with independent people who are going to come
on the lot to make a movie, and they tend to respect

them more as filmmakers than in the old days when the studios had contract producers. They didn't care a shit then who you liked or who you didn't like. But I think a lot of that has changed and very much for the better.

● *You're preparing a film with Burt Reynolds, right? Do you think that by using him you are guaranteed a certain success?*

I consider Burt Reynolds a very talented actor. I remember Burt way back at Universal. I go back with Burt—not as a friend, but watching his career—a long way. He's done some very good work, but more than anything else the most exciting thing about Burt is that he is a showman. I don't care what form of publicity he may generate, if it's *Cosmopolitan* or involved in a murder. Today you see pictures of actors digging in the garden with the wife and kids and they're "everyman," but Burt—Burt Reynolds is bigger than life! Burt has glamour.

● *Isn't that what's lacking in most of the actors today?*

I think that's exactly what's lacking, and I think that's why he's so successful.

● *What about the women? Lately there's been a lot of static from women about the fact that there are no women's roles for anybody over twenty-four except when they're some sort of sex object. If there is a picture that requires a woman star you say, "Who the hell am I going to get to play it?"*

That's true. I've been involved with the Gwen Davis book *Kingdom Come*. There are two major female parts—younger girls. There are maybe three or four actresses with merit who have any value or any recognizable name. It's very tough. I think the whole thing that happened to women in the motion picture business would make a very interesting book.

71

● *What did happen?*

It's very interesting. We came out of World War II, and we were still into the star system. Remember what we talked about earlier, what the people talk about today when they talk about films and what they talked about then. Motion pictures were made, conceived, and financed much more then than now on who the major stars were. OK. When World War II was over and Hollywood went back into major production, they started hanging on all the stars that were around *before* the war—Burt Lancaster, Kirk Douglas, Jimmy Stewart, John Wayne. You name them; they were the major male stars that were around before the war. The major female stars? They were now all older women and couldn't play leading ladies anymore. Gary Cooper, a man of fifty, fifty-five years old, was playing in a love story with Audrey Hepburn! Unfortunately, biology was destiny with Hollywood on that level, and the major female stars—they got married and got out of the business like Greer Garson, or, just due to the fact that a forty- to fifty-year-old woman couldn't get into a story with a twenty-five-year-old guy, it was lopsided by the way we were conditioned to expect older-younger people to relate.

The big turning point was that we needed the stars to make the movies and there were no major female stars. Ingrid Bergman was maybe the last, along with Susan Hayward and Rita Hayworth. Don't forget Kirk Douglas is still working, but those women can't work as major stars in the United States. When the studio was viable and it was producing, the female stars were almost a more stable commodity—the Irene Dunnes, the Myrna Loys, the Claudette Colberts—they were more viable in this business than the men were. And when that structure collapsed, who were you going to develop?

● *Do you think this problem exists because the business is run by a lot of insecure males who, maybe subconsciously, are scared of a woman having an important role in the industry?*

You talk to agents and you talk to producers; they traditionally are a little wary of developing a female star for a lot of reasons. For one, they ultimately think a woman is going to get married, have a lot of kids, and walk out. That's the mentality, right? Two, they get a girl like a Marilyn Monroe, sell her as a sex symbol and a sexpot, and five years go by and she's not. Whereas if you get a Steve McQueen and develop him, you've got thirty years of him playing exactly the same character. You have different factors at work and in a dollars-and-cents society it vindicates itself; I've heard it discussed a thousand times. Listen, I did a film called *Little Fauss and Big Halsey* with Robert Redford, Michael Pollard, and Lauren Hutton. Paramount had an option on Lauren Hutton that had to be exercised one year after the start of the film. They liked Lauren, they really did, but they didn't have a movie for her.

● *What has happened to her since then? Has she gone on working as an actress?*

Yes, a couple of films, one being *The Gambler,* and now she's the Revson girl and makes a fortune—much more than she can ever make in movies. But look at the number of women who have come and gone, really hit big and have never sustained it. That's really kind of frightening, and, let's be honest, nobody's writing scripts for women, either, so one thing feeds the other.

Because of the fact there are so few female stars, you don't want to get involved with a piece of material which deals with female stars. And because you're not developing that kind of material, there's less opportunity to develop the stars. It all gets twisted together and you can't bust out. I guess the only major star that's happened in the United States has been Goldie Hawn out of television. I think what we said about Burt Reynolds—that show biz, glamour, a flair, that he's bigger than life—if a girl walked in with that quality and you worked on that, you'd have a major female star.

● *Marilyn Monroe, when she started. . .*

She was under contract.

● *So what we're saying is that if she started today you wouldn't look at her twice? You've really got to take somebody and say, "I see in that person that germ of glamour," and then nurture it along?*

Yes, but with how the business exists today, tell me who is supposed to do that. It will be more incumbent on the actor to do more for himself than he used to do under the old studio system. They've got to get an image of themselves and improve themselves. It's true; there has been a vacuum created by a collapse of the major studios, at least in that area, the area of developing talent. But there'll always be new faces; new faces are going to break through always and I don't care if there are no studios or we go back tomorrow to a studio system. Nobody manufactured Clark Gable, no one. You may accent and develop him along, but Clark Gable was Clark Gable, and Burt Reynolds is Burt Reynolds, and Clint Eastwood is Clint Eastwood. Obviously, the actor has to sustain and develop himself and project his image and fight for the opportunities. It was much easier in the old days, but the rewards are greater today for the actor to make money and get the power and the ultimate ego trip of doing what he really wants to do. Far greater today.

● *What would impress you if an actor or an actress walked through that door? Looks, background—what?*

When I meet a girl, for instance, the first thing that hits me is what she looks like. I don't mean she has to be gorgeous or this or that, but the first impression triggers off something in you—how she walks, how she talks, what she's saying, and where you think her head is at. You may find out later that there are other things that make her more or less attractive, but generally, on the skin, people are what they are. I don't care about somebody's credits if they're not major credits. I'll put it this way—if Al Pacino walks in and he's won the Obie Award and the Tony Award on and off Broadway two consecutive years, that's very impressive to me. Not that I would automatically hire somebody because of that. But that's an impressive credit for anybody. For an actor to walk in and say, "I did *Streetcar Named Desire* at the Nashville Playhouse"—I would then go strongly on my intuitive feelings. And I do believe in screen tests.

● *When you tested for the parts James Caan and Al Pacino played in* The Godfather, *how did you arrive at these actors? Did you have a concept of what you wanted, and did they fit the parts better than anybody else or what?*

What you do is you break down. You get to the core of what each part is. For Sonny we needed someone who had rages, a physicality, a certain humor, big balls— you get all the parameters set in, what a part is about.

You might find two actors who could conceivably fill these qualifications, but then you'll probably find one actor who will fill them a little better.

When I first met Mario Puzo, who wrote the book, he said, "You know there's only one guy who should play the godfather, and that's Brando." I felt like telling him, "Look, don't tell me how to run my business; just keep writing." And we forgot about it until I got together with the director, Francis Ford Coppola, and the subject of Brando came up again. The reason we ended up wanting him is very interesting. The godfather is in the book and in the film thirty or thirty-three percent of the time, but he's a man whose mystique and power permeate the whole thing. You're always aware of the man, so we needed a man who had the mystique and the power of a Brando. What other actor could bring you that? I mean the guy does have a mystique. No one knows anything about Brando except they all think he's wierd or this or that. That worked for us; that's why he was such a natural choice. He's mysterious; he's inaccessible; the guy is a very bizarre human being with enormous power. And he intimidates people, not that he means to, but it's unavoidable, and that's what the character of Don Corleone was.

● *How was he working with other actors? How did he relate to them personally and professionally?*

The thing about Brando is that he's the greatest actor in the world to work with. The first day of read-throughs all the actors were in the rehearsal hall before Marlon showed, and they were all laughing. Jimmy Caan was doing his routine; Richard Castellano and Bobby Duvall were having fun; then the door opened and in walked Marlon. Everyone froze! The first time Al Pacino worked with Brando in *The Godfather* was when he comes to the hospital and wheels the bed out. I'm on the set and I see Al standing there, stumbling, and I say, "Are you OK? What the hell's wrong with you?" He replied, "Do you know what it means to me to finally be doing a scene with Marlon Brando? I studied acting for fifteen years; I've seen every movie this man has made twenty times; and, my God, now I'm doing a scene with him." It's like an architect working with Frank Lloyd Wright. Marlon intimidated all the actors for about a half-hour. But the man has a marvelous sense of humor; he's very generous and really had to work to break the other actors down. They were so overwhelmed by him until he got them to relax. Every actor on the film loved him; he was terrific with all of them.

● *Is he professional with punctuality, lines, and so on?*

Look, maybe he's ready with his lines and maybe he isn't. The thing that's so great about him is that he plays the part so much more than it was ever written in the script. Like there were so many things that he did in *The Godfather* that weren't in the script. The man is so inventive on a textural level. There were hundreds of things he did in that film that may have seemed insignificant, but when you start totaling all those things, it gave the man an amazing texture. Even when he became an old man it wasn't brilliant makeup; it's that he understood the quality, the abstract and essence of old age. He played the senility, not lines. Obviously, you can't train somebody to be an actor like that. Someone is either an actor or he isn't. You can learn the craft, but you can't make somebody an actor. Also, there's something about certain people that you can't take your eyes off. You like to watch them; they're interesting to watch; they make interesting choices of certain lines that other actors would do nothing with. There are an awful lot of shticks and tricks, but certain people just have great intuitive sense.

It takes time for some people. Burt Reynolds, for example, could have been a giant ten years ago had he got the right chance—say if Burt was in *Butch Cassidy*. We have to hang in there for the right breaks, and sometimes it takes longer than others. I don't feel Burt Reynolds is any more talented today than he was ten years ago, but he's more interesting as a man. I think there comes a moment that is *your* time, if you're a producer, a director, a writer, or an actor. Like with Bill Inge, the playwright. He was "where it was at" and then five or ten years later couldn't sell anything.

● *When you said you'd been in the computer business, that you'd been an architect and a land developer, then wanted to get into this business, how did you go about it?*

I always wanted to be a producer, but didn't have the funds or the connections. I therefore felt there was no opportunity for me to be a producer except with a good piece of material. So I tried finding a piece of material, and without money you get all the shlock scripts that everyone's passed over. So I decided to become a writer. I would write something that they would let me produce because they wanted the material. That's why I started working with Bernie Fein as a writer and actually did very well with "Hogan's Heroes." After that I told Paramount three story ideas. I didn't have them written down, didn't have a treatment, a star, a synopsis, a director, book, or anything. I don't think

Albert S. Ruddy

anyone else has ever done this, but it's really a wild story. One was *Little Fauss,* and one was the film I'm doing now with Burt Reynolds. That's one of the original stories. But I've hung in there, I must say—five years.

● *Do you think the main prerequisite is having the goal, really wanting it badly?*

Rightfully or wrongfully we are living in a goal-oriented society; that's where it's at. But hanging in there is what it's all about. Everyone has a goal, and everyone has to figure out how to get through the eye of the needle. I guess I'm a true neurotic, because there was never a doubt in my mind that I would make it—finis. Don't ask me why. I didn't know that much, and there were certainly a lot more people who were far more experienced and talented, but I had that absolute, total belief that whatever I put my mind to I would make it. There was no question that I couldn't, and so it was very easy. When you see the people who are making it, they're not exactly the giants of the Western World. There are a lot of imbeciles in this business who are big and powerful people. I'd be sitting on the wrong side of the desk and I'd be thinking, "Hm, how come I'm on this side and he's on the other?" I'm as great as I am depending on who the other guys are who are competing with me for what I want to do. And if they seem and look that much better than me, then I'm on the low end of the totem pole. And if I'm really that much better than them, I'm on the top. It's all relative.

# Susan Anspach
## Actress

## "My first agent I married!"

Susan Anspach was born in New York City and attended Bryant School in Long Island City. She also attended Catholic University of America in Washington, D.C., where she got her degree in drama. She is married to actor Mark Goddard and is the mother of two children. In New York, on and off Broadway, she appeared in the following plays:

*A View from the Bridge*
*Journey of the Fifth Horse*
*A Midsummer Night's Dream*
*Ninety Day Mistress*
*The Lover*
*Things That Go Bump in the Night*
*Hair*
*Viveca Lindfors' Education Tour of the Classics*
*And All That Jazz*

Films
*The Landlord*
*Five Easy Pieces*
*Play It Again, Sam*
*Blume in Love*

Susan Anspach came to our office wearing the same baggy dungarees and "half-off, half-on" blouse that she'd probably worn to her audition for *Five Easy Pieces*. As we looked at her—thinner than thin, seemingly timid, with pretty natural blond hair to her waist—we both had the feeling we'd have rather a tough time dragging anything worthwhile out of this young actress. We were wrong. No sooner had we turned on the tape recorder and asked our first question than she was off. It didn't seem necessary for us to phrase the questions at all. Without any trouble we realized why Susan is becoming one of the hottest young actresses in the industry. She has a quality and the drive of a bulldozer, and she is overflowing with confidence. She's got all the things it takes to succeed in this business.

● *How did you come to Hollywood?*

It was a very practical thing that brought me out here. I knew I could be more of a full-time mother and I could support my child better if I were living in Los Angeles compared to New York, where the money you get for a play is so little and the time you have to put into it is so great. Out here, if I were to do a movie or one television show, I could support us fine. I could have a nurse on the set with me and could even run out and nurse my child in between shots. The money would be sufficient to support us three and four months at a time—that was my idea. It was strictly that, and it turned out to be fantastic.

● *What made you want to become an actress, and how did you get started?*

As a child I lived with great emotions and drama—a supersized life. That, combined with the fact that I was very religious, made me unconsciously lean toward acting. Besides being a victim, like the rest of American girls, you want to be a star. You want to be beautiful and have everyone pay attention to you. Stanislavski even calls a theater a temple, and a church for me was a place of great ritual, great excitement, and great fantasy.

Consciously, I went to college to do something very humanitarian. I wanted to be a lawyer or a politician, someone who really does something for society. From childhood I knew I had to do something worthwhile and, like most women who know they have to get married, that was not part of my life. I went to the Catholic University of America because of my religion, but the college I chose happened to be very famous for its drama department. I loved singing and music; music was the happiest part of my childhood. Because I sang, somebody said, "Why don't you try out for this play. None of the actresses can do it because you have to sing, and there's not too much acting." So I tried and got the part and realized that although intellectually I wanted all these other things, psychologically I really wanted a place to express all those emotional things I'd been feeling all my life. So I became an actress.

● *Once you decided to become an actress, what did you do next?*

I switched majors; I got my degree in drama. Then I went to New York. That's where I was born and raised, so it was the logical place to go rather than Los Angeles. That summer I did the things that most actresses do but with such fanaticism that it really worked for me. I took the trades. The trades out here aren't good for casting, et cetera, but the trades in New York are really good for casting. For example, Equity has something that the Screen Actors Guild doesn't have which is terrific, and that's how I got my first job. It's called an "open call," a non-Equity audition. The director, whether he wants to or not, has to audition anybody and everybody who comes that day. I was like number eighty-nine and got it. It was off-Broadway.

Now to go back a little. I'm very mathematical, very orderly. I keep a lot of lists, appointment books, and things like that. I made a list of the auditions that were open each day and went to every one of them, making sure I had a job from four P.M. till twelve midnight. I was supervisor of the maids at the New York Hilton. Any job that goes late in the afternoon is fine, because you've got the morning and midafternoon for auditions. At that time, I was studying with Herbert Berghof. He said an interesting thing to me, which I had known from college. I was not considered a good actress at all; it was scary. Herbert said to me, "You're one of the most talented students I have, but I don't know whether you'll be able to act." So I said, "Well, I guess I'd better go find a teacher that can teach me." What he meant was this: An artist needs to have a lot of soul, a lot of emotion, and I think that's what he saw, but not craft. I had extreme nervous energy but an incapacity to express what was going on inside.

So I called up Sandy Meisner. Sandy took me on as a student, and it was just a matter of two or three months of his technique and I was able to get out of that kind of frightening shell that every time I walked on stage it was, "Oh, God, save me; I can't stand it." Sandy did it with three things that we should all live our lives by. One was that nothing worse than catastrophe can happen, and if catastrophe happens, so what? That's the worst it's going to be. So you fall down on your face, so you forget your lines—so what? He had this amazing capacity to make you realize that really it was OK to be lousy. Two, an ounce of behavior is worth a pound of words. He took the emphasis off lines. In college they really emphasized lines, and that hangs any new actor up. If you have to start thinking that you have to say the right thing the right way at the right time, your attention is focused on something you yet can't deal with. Three, "Act before you think." For me, who is very competitive intellectually, this took all the fear, all the pressure of having to do a good intellectual job of acting and analyzing. Meaning: As an actor does something and it creates an impulse in you, do that impulse. Don't think about it; don't think, "Is it right or wrong for the character?" And it works. Amazingly, for me it worked immediately.

Very shortly after, I auditioned for this off-Broadway play, *A View from the Bridge*, and the assistant director was Dustin Hoffman. The people who starred in it were Bobby Duvall and Jon Voight. The director and Dustin liked me, so I came back to audition for Arthur Miller and got the part.

● *How long ago was this?*

Eight years ago. Then I did a Broadway play called *Things That Go Bump in the Night*, starring Eileen Heckart and Bobby Drivas. It was a disaster—Broadway's all-time worst play. I was in terrible fights with the director, and Equity had to come and get me out of my apartment with the threat of suspending me for a year if I didn't do it. Luckily for me, *View from the Bridge* ran for two years, and the director, who was very fond of me, allowed me to keep going in and out of it so if I did a flop I could go back to *View from the Bridge*. I did mostly drama at that time, very heavy things. As Lee Strasberg says, a beginning artist starts by imitating, and that's a good way to start. You use it as a point of departure. And so I was either playing Kim Stanley or Sandy Dennis. I was either weeping and trying to be very heavy or I was very kooky and very neurotic, and these were the parts I played.

In January of 1966 I auditioned for the Actors Studio and, at that time, it was a very prestigious thing. Out of eleven hundred people, seven got in. I got in and worked with a lot of interesting people—Al Pacino, et cetera—but the most interesting thing I did was an aria, which is what I ultimately want to do. Stanislavski, before he died, started directing opera. He felt the highest place to go in theater was to do opera because you could totally express yourself. He felt that talking was an abortion of real expression—a repression, an offense against really being expressive. I study opera twice a week right now. It was great working with the studio. I did a lot of varied things.

● *Did you continue at the West Coast Studio when you came out to Hollywood?*

A little, but it isn't a very healthy atmosphere. Los Angeles in general is not a good atmosphere for actors, but I've changed my life style so much out here. I'm a mother and a wife.

There's a fantastic article I read by a psychologist. He discussed creativity, not hypothetically but empirically. You set up the problem and a million different answers for the problem, and you go through torture trying to find the right answer. Now in my case specifically—a key to an acting problem—you just throw out the whole problem and say, "To hell with that. I don't care about problems. I'm going to go on to something else." And after you've thrown it away the answer just comes. Now the answer wouldn't have come if you hadn't worked that hard at solving the problem, but it also wouldn't have come if you hadn't given up solving the problem. This happened to me as an actress; although I think I acted well in New York, I don't think the key to solving a lot of my problems as an actress came until I almost gave it up. Acting to me was terribly secondary by the time I came out here. Having my child, loving her, and being a mother was really all that mattered.

● *When you got to Hollywood, what were the steps you took to get an agent?*

My first agent I married! An actor friend of mine was interested in my finding a good agent. He had a friend call several agents, and I met this one man who was working for Phil Gersh—Mark Goddard. He really wasn't an agent but an actor and in some despair had become an agent for a few months. I met him, and he was very good for me because he loved my talent. I guess the combination of my New York credentials and his kind on enthusiasm—well, I was "in like Flynn." It was amazing, but there wasn't a film that had a part that I could play that I didn't either screen test for or wasn't offered. I just turned everything down until I did *The Landlord,* and that I did because I liked Hal Ashby, the director. I keep turning things down until I find a part I'm interested in doing. The scripts I do want to do much come my way, but there are not too many of them. I hope I'll be offered enough good scripts that I'll be able to do one or two a year that I like.

There are not too many parts written for women, but they are beginning to demand good actresses. The ones that studied hard in New York *are* actresses, and the ones that came directly to Los Angeles, I believe, came out here to be stars—to make it on their looks and charm. But it's beginning to happen for women as it did for men—the Dustin Hoffmans, Bobby Duvalls, Al Pacinos, and even Elliott Gould for a while. People like that came out here because they did all their hard work in New York and they made sure they knew a little bit about acting before they exposed themselves to the public. Now the same is happening with women.

One of the problems is that men are writing the scripts and men are directing them. A man will still use a woman that he's attracted to. For example, Mike Nichols used Candice Bergen and Ann-Margaret in *Carnal Knowledge.* Either it was a combination of being attracted to these women or having some kind of Svengali attitude of taking a nonactress type and making her act. In fact, Mike Nichols was then going with Candy Bergen.

● *After you've reached a certain point in your career, do you think it's necessary to leave the small agent and sign with a larger agency in order to get powerful representation?*

Unfortunately, I think it is. I'm a person who highly regards fidelity, loyalty, and all those things, but I just don't think the smaller agent can handle it. For example, I was with a small agent when *Five Easy Pieces* came out, and you'd think, "God, he helped get her that? What kind of lack of fidelity is it not to stay with him?" Well, I did stay, and he was trying to put me in television shows, et cetera. But, I'm sorry, for me there's a policy out here. If you do a series or a guest star in a series at a certain point in your career, it's considered backsliding and you can't do it. And the little agent has a way of being afraid; they have to pay the dollars and cents; their bills come in every month. CMA can wait a year, but a small agency that's going to get you $3,500 for one week's shooting or $15,000 for a television movie is going to want you to do it. That means a lot of money to them. I'd get pushed around by a small agency, whereas a big agency knows how to protect me.

● *How did you get the female lead in* Blume in Love?
   Paul Mazursky, the director, saw me in *Five Easy
   Pieces*. He thought it was the most truthful performance by a woman he'd seen.
● *So how did you get* Five Easy Pieces?
   For *Five Easy Pieces* I auditioned for the part of Rayette,
   the part eventually played by Karen Black. Bob
   Rafelson, the director, was very interested in me for it. I
   came into the office. Mark, my first agent who was by
   this time my husband, had given me this great
   confidence to be myself. To digress a moment, the first
   thing one agent said to me was, "You've got to change
   that name. How about Susan Adams?" It was like that
   with most agents, but Mark was so sure I was the female
   Jimmy Dean, that the more I was myself the better off
   I'd be. And that's a good lesson for actors: Absolutely be
   yourself. I'd go into offices (I was then nursing my
   child, and, because I couldn't afford a baby sitter, my
   baby went with me on all my auditions) and in the
   middle of the interview I'd say, "Excuse me," and turn
   around and put her under my bra and nurse her, then
   turn to continue the interview. It was just so natural
   that it made me relaxed and independent. People like
   that. It was like, "You want me for the part? You don't?
   Goodbye!" And it's a very good place to be.
      So I came in to audition for Rayette, and as Bob
   Rafelson describes it now, I came in with baggy
   dungarees and a blouse that was half on and half off and
   a kid under my arm. I seemed perfect for the part of
   Rayette, so we started off auditioning. By the second
   reading he started giving me direction which I tried to
   follow. About halfway through I finally said, "You
   know something, Bob; I like you a lot, but don't think
   we're going to get along. I'm very opinionated, strong-

willed, and my life is in a good place right now, full of
good vibrations. If I do this part, we're going to get into
fights because we don't see eye to eye on it. It was nice
meeting you. Good luck in finding the girl." And I left.
He called me up three weeks later: "Well, seeing you
don't want to play the lead in my movie, would you
consider another part—Katherine?" "Sounds good," I
said, and that was it. I still get comments like, "You
were so perfectly cast in *Five Easy Pieces.*"

● *Is it true that in Hollywood you're either an actress or a
star?*

Oddly enough, yes. On the screen, the person—that
part of his or her personality, that "star quality," rather
than all the other things he or she creates up there—
seems to be larger. The screen is so big and so truthful.
Liv Ullmann, I'm sure, is quite plain in a room, but put
that camera on her, and something incredible happens.
Her own depth and her own stillness, all her sensitivity
adds so much to that screen that who cares if somebody
else can act it as well? You're seeing that "star quality."
You may not have it in your personal life, but when
you're acting you have to have it once you get on that
stage or that screen. Dustin Hoffman and I were sitting
in the Gaiety Delicatessen during rehearsals for *View
from the Bridge.* Dustin said to me, "If I were a little
older, I'd be playing Bobby Duvall's part. I'm a
brilliant actor." Dusty was the plainest person; you'd
never think he had any charm, any of that special
"lights going on." But God, once he started acting you
just went, "Wow!"

● *Do you find it difficult to work with an actor that you
don't know personally?*

Every actor is different about that, especially the
English actors. I'm sure a Glenda Jackson has strictly

done her homework from the script, not from the other human beings. Most English actors do that. Method acting is a different technique, and it really depends on what technique works for you. I personally need to know the other person. It creates the necessary sympathy, vibrancy, et cetera, that I don't believe the other way of working does.

● *Have you ever worked with an actor closely, respected him as an actor, but just couldn't work well with him?*

Yes, that's called substitution. According to the method, you trick your mind to think that that's a different person—somebody that you sympathize with—rather than the actor you're working with. If you do your homework—get all that going—and also work off the other person, then you've really got it.

● *How did you like working with Paul Mazursky as a director on* Blume in Love?

Paul was fantastic. He's almost like a businessman in his capacity to create an extremely relaxed atmosphere.

● *Was he helpful in guiding you with qualities and depths in your character?*

It's hard for me to know in this particular role; I felt so close to the character. His contribution to me was his total trust and willingness to go with whatever I did, which was not necessarily what he wrote. Many people who read the script didn't like it nearly as much as the movie. People who read it told Paul to go with Ali MacGraw or Candice Bergen. They read her as a very cold woman. I played it differently.

● *Have you found the satisfaction that you hoped to achieve and that made you want to be an actress?*

Extremely. Extraordinarily. I had a director in New York say, "Susan, of all the people I've met you'll never become an alcoholic, a drug addict, or anything like that, because I've never seen anyone get so stoned on his work." Acting for me is a place to go, a temple, a whole being. For example, before I start acting, I do relaxation exercises. I purge myself out of my daily existence. I get rid of trivia and become one with the character, one with the moment. I try desperately to make this moment *now*. One tends to think, "Oh, I've got this appointment. Oh, I didn't get the dishes done." One's life can be so full of trivia. Life is utilitarian or it isn't, and I'm capable of being nonutilitarian as an actress. In church you're nonutilitarian; you're living a highly emotional state. Acting is incredible for me that way, and I don't want it to come off sounding as therapy either. It's not therapy; it's beauty. It's a beautiful place to go.

You asked me before about working with the other actor. I find it's a religious experience to act with somebody in film. When I work with another actor, I expose myself completely. That's why I get in fights with directors. It's that while I'm acting, I'm so vulnerable in order to respond totally to this other human being that I can't bear someone else coming in on that wavelength.

● *In your profession do you wish to communicate something to the audience?*

I'm not sure I think or care about the fact that people get any kind of message out of watching me or how much they are inspired or enlightened. I think my art is quite selfish in that respect, and I know why. It's kind of bitter, but I don't trust the audience. They have to go out and look at themselves before I can do them any good. In other words, the same audience that put the senators off the air and made Archie Bunker number one—I can't deal with that. I can't worry about them getting any beauty or trip out of me. They have to do that for themselves.

● *Doesn't the mere fact that you're making a film mean you're trying to communicate?*

No. That's the thing I'm saying. The moment of acting is what's basic, what's important to me. The film is just an excuse to act.

● *You say you are very careful with the material that you select. Do you think most actors are capable of reading a script and evaluating it?*

I think I have to be more humble about that. For example, I didn't show up for an audition last week for the film based on the book *The Day of the Locust*. I don't want to do a film about old Hollywood and degenerates. I want to do more things like *Love Story*, poetic things. If I had my way I'd do a talkie of *City Lights* with Woody Allen.

● *If you admired the director greatly, would this influence you to do a film even though you did not care much for the script?*

Yes, if I admired him in terms of ethics and morals. For example, there's a certain director—I saw a picture of his and said, "I'd never work for that man. He's unethical and he hates women." So I wouldn't care if it were *Alice in Wonderland* and he wanted me to play Alice. I wouldn't trust doing a film with him. The same thing goes for the opposite. I like Alan Pakula. I think he has fantastic morals and I think he works marvelously with women. He has an uncanny way of finding something in women that you care about. I think if I read a script and didn't particularly care for it, I would trust that he had something beyond what I cound see in it.

● *How do you feel about taking your clothes off?*

Terrible. I would never do it. It doesn't advance the story, and it doesn't advance the part—to the contrary. You look up and you say, "Hm, I didn't know that actress had a beautiful bosom," or, "Gee, she doesn't have any wrinkles in her thighs yet," or, "I wonder if she felt embarrassed doing that." You think things that have absolutely nothing to do with the movie or the plot. It takes you right out of it from the audience point of view. It has no logic to me. It's dumb and it's ugly!

● *Where do you feel the film industry is headed?*

I'm really depressed about it. People are now saying to me, "You're really in, Susan. It's really your time, because they're starting to do women's parts and women's films." But their idea of a woman's part is some gum-chewing, liberated, bossy, bitchy, horrible woman. Either that or an absolutely crazy woman about ready to kill herself. Well, I don't mind killing myself for Tennessee Williams or Arthur Miller, but there's very little excuse for being in most films today. Most of them are just being done to make a lot of money. The chairman of the board of some high-powered business running a studio today wants to brag about making a lot of money, not being attached to something that's a good, artistic picture.

● *Do you think luck has any part in the career of an actor, being at the right place at the right time?*

Yes. I think it takes great will power and drive to do it, but then you can have great will power and great drive and still not make it.

# Aaron Spelling

## Executive Producer

"I tell you, I used to almost cry when I didn't get a part."

Aaron Spelling was born in Dallas, Texas, attended Southern Methodist University, and studied at the Sorbonne in Paris, France. While at S.M.U. he received the Harvard Award for the best original one-act play. He moved from school straight into staging plays at the Margo Jones Theatre and the Dallas Little Theatre. In 1953 Aaron came to Hollywood, where he was first a success as an actor. He continued writing and eventually went on to great success as a producer of television series and "Movies of the Week."

Among his credits as producer are the following:

"Johnny Ringo"
"Zane Grey Theatre"
"Dick Powell Show"
"Kaiser Presents the Lloyd Bridges Show"
"The June Allyson Show"
"The Smothers Brothers Show"
"Burke's Law"
"Honey West"

In partnership with Danny Thomas:

"The Danny Thomas Hour"
"The Guns of Will Sonnett"
"Movies of the Week"
"Mod Squad"

Aaron Spelling Productions:

23 "Movies of the Week"
"The Rookies"
"S.W.A.T."

Twentieth Century-Fox Studios was quite dead except for the pickets at the gate. The writers were on strike. Aaron Spelling kept us waiting an hour in his elaborate offices in the executive bungalow, but he bounced in and was most apologetic. He had been scouting locations for one of his TV shows. He is extremely thin, with large eyes and long, bony hands. It all adds up to an offbeat attractiveness. Having been an actor himself, his whole life revolving around this business, he has an intense interest in and a sympathetic attitude toward the people who have not yet made it. Though he has many matters to attend to in the course of one day, he closed off his phones and gave us his complete attention. As we both walked out of the building, we wondered why many people don't like Aaron as much as we had on that first meeting!

● *You started out as an actor. How did you become a producer?*

I came out here, strangely enough, as a director. I'd been producing summer stock in Dallas, Texas. From there I went to New York as a director and finally came out here and was signed by Columbia. Because of a writers' strike, all the studios closed up, and I was starving to death. I directed a play. Jack Webb came to see it and said, "I wish I could use you as a director, but I have the director signed. Are you an actor?" I said, "Yes." I think I did more "Dragnet"s than any actor in history. A series of "Dragnet"s was done by three people: Charlie Bronson, Lee Marvin, and myself. I played all the pyromaniacs, and they played all the maniacal rapists. I loved acting, but I knew myself, and physically there was only a certain amount I could do. I would never be a Rock Hudson. What I really wanted to do was write. All my life I'd wanted to write, and all the time I was acting I was writing. The producers and directors I met as an actor were the ones that bought my first scripts. I wrote fifty-five television shows, including "Playhouse 90," before I became a producer.

● *Do you think that an actor has a better chance if he is not a definite type?*

Yes; he has a better chance of longevity, and he has a better chance at better roles. But I think it depends on your own psyche—where you want to go. I was a very ambitious young guy.

● *Do you think you could play a leading man today?*

No.

● *What about Charles Bronson? Charles Bronson plays leading men.*

Charles Bronson has a strange, physical, vulgar sex

appeal that really appeals to European audiences, not to American audiences. I remember Charlie when the only parts he could get were Indians. Charlie was so disgusted with America that he went to Europe. In Europe they go crazy for Charlie. They love him. He's one of their biggest guys. He gets $500,000 a picture. Lee Van Cleef is a huge star over there. Lee Van Cleef came back to do *The Second Ride of the Magnificent Seven,* a disastrous bomb, a secondary, cheap western, for the Mirisch brothers here. They shot it in eight days—pure trash. He went back to Italy, where he's a star, and said, "To hell with Hollywood!"

Most of the actors that I know were like me. I got a job taking airline reservations at Western Airlines or in a restaurant hauling trays, and then as a mail boy at KTTV—and that's where I find most of my actors. I meet actors who park my car. "I'm an actor," they say. "Can I come to see you?" And you know what? If they're attractive enough and cute enough and bright enough—when I say "attractive," I don't mean pretty people at all, but if there's a personality—those are the people I see. I admire the fact that they're working their tails off and they're struggling to stay alive and they have a personality. There's an attraction for people like that. We all like con men in a way. It's an art really. They're con men basically, selling their own personality. That's all they have to sell. That's why they're hurt so much.

● *Having been an actor yourself, how do you feel having to turn someone down for a part?*

It bothers me. When I say no to an actor or an actress, what I really mean is, "God, dear, I'm sorry you're not really right for this role, and I love you. You're dear, but I have to say no." What unfortunately happens is the agent talks to the casting director, and he says, "Sorry, we don't think he's right." The agent then calls up the actor and says, "You weren't right." That person now has been terribly rejected, because all that they've sold is their face and their personality, and they think, "I'm too pretty; I'm too ugly; I'm too tall; I'm too short; I'm too fat, too thin; I've sold my flesh. And he didn't like me. Why didn't he like me? What's wrong with me?" I tell you, I used to almost cry when I didn't get a part. Not because I needed the money that desperately, but it's that personal rejection. When they rejected my scripts, my attitude was, "Screw you," and I'd gotten paid for it.

● *As one of the biggest television producers in the business, do you get many queries from aspiring actors?*

Most of the time it starts with letters saying, "I'm graduating from such and such a university; what do I do to get started as an actor in Hollywood?" They literally think you come to Hollywood, pick up the phone, get an agent, and the agent gets you in pictures. That's all there is to it! I've seen so many people come out here with a hundred dollars, pay their month's rent, get photographs, and then they're destitute. They get caught in so many schemes. Photographers tell them, "You must have pictures." Hell, you don't need pictures. If you don't have an agent, who are you going to show the pictures to? Horrible! Horrible! Another scheme is: "We will make you a videotape and will get you work." Well, they're not going to get you jobs, and the tapes are disgusting. In the first few weeks, which is the hardest period, you feel like everybody in Hollywood's a phony. You feel like it's an impenetrable city and it's made out of concrete and you'll never get in—but there are some basic rules.

I had a nephew who lived in San Francisco. He wanted to be an actor, and he said, "Uncle Aaron, what do I do?" I told him, "The first thing you do is have enough money or get yourself a job, because you're going to be hurt and you may not work for six months." The next thing I did was to tell him to drive around the city, get to know the place, 'cause you'll go crazy. Hollywood's such a small town and we only have five or six studios, and if you know where they are, it makes you feel part of the community. Then the next thing is get into an acting group. If you're an actor you've got to act! At least that can be a place where, even if it doesn't happen too often, maybe a casting director will see you. I have a casting director that goes to theater about once every two weeks, but I must admit I don't. Off the record, I get so hurt when I see these poor kids knocking their brains out. If they know there's a producer in the audience, you always get a note from the manager of the theater saying, "Can we talk to you afterwards?"

I would also advise any young actor to use any influence he has, to use college professors to write a casting director and say, "Would you just see him?" The problem the actors have is getting seen. There's a young guy in "The Rookies," Michael Ontkean. He's staggering. You probably saw the fan mail outside. He's Canadian, and he knew of Norman Jewison, who was also Canadian, and called him up—like, "I'm an actor, could you get me in?" Jewison called me, and I saw him, and that was that. I think to be a young actor you must first look for a contact, know the area you want to break through and work at it, read the trades. There are open meetings of the Screen Actors Guild, open meetings of the Television Academy. Try to join, to be, to go. That sounds like an old Hollywood cliché,

but it's true. I tell you that in the heyday of the Daisy
Club there were more actors cast at that club than there
were at the studio.

● *Do you think it's easier for a girl to get a role that way
because girls get invited to parties and so on?*
Then we're talking about that very special cosmetic
look, and that's so hard to find. I haven't seen what I
would call a staggering, special-looking girl since
Candice Bergen. If you're that way, you're not going to
have any trouble. Unfortunately, the cosmetic beauties
famous in Hollywood today are, say, two percent. I
don't think anybody would say Steve McQueen looks
like a young Tony Curtis—he looks like a bike
mechanic—but there's a look. Unless you have that very
special look, you're really wasting your time with
pictures and things. You must join a group, find an
agent, meet some casting directors. There are still a lot
of casting directors who will see people, and I find that
if you write—very strange trick—write a very intelligent letter to a casting director, tell him who you are,
what you've done, *be honest.* Tell him you know how
busy he is and would he give you five minutes. I think
that approach may work.

● *Can the actor get any further than the casting directors?*
I think there are casting directors who will read an
actor, and if he's interesting, will come to me. I've had
two casting directors, Betty Martin and Bert Remsen,
and they've both said to me at one time or another, "Has
no credits but there's something there," and you quite
possibly use them.

● *Do you look at much TV in order to discover new faces?*
All the time. We also don't cast by rote. Once we've got a
script, we're ready to shoot, and we've got nineteen
parts that we've got to cast. I would say that we see

about ninety-five people. We read about eighteen girls at least before we cast a part. And when we're doing a series—say "The Rookies"—at least a couple of hundred kids.

● *On your show "The Rookies," for instance, if you hire an actor for a one-line part and he comes over well, will you bring him back for a larger role?*

I can name you three actors this year. One of the kids we put in a lead in one of the "Rookies" segments. His first role was in a small part in "The Rookies." In the last "Rookies" of the year he was the lead, and because of that he got a series—a black actor called Hilly Elkins. And that happens all the time.

● *Is it easier for an unknown actor to get a television series?*

That's a good question. Sometimes. We go through periods. It used to be that you couldn't get a series unless you were a star. Now I think it depends on the show. I think there are two types of series—one where you walk in and say, "I have Cary Grant, who's going to do the series," or a show like "Mod Squad" or "The Rookies" where they like the concept so much they really want unknowns. Much more beneficial to go with unknowns, and I can name five or six series like that.

● *So the young actors really have a chance today?*

Gosh, yes. I think even more so. Putting great actors in bad concepts results in bad TV. The Jimmy Stewart series was a terrible disaster. There was not a better actor in the world than Jimmy Stewart. Henry Fonda in "The Smith Family" was a terrible disaster. There's not a better actor in the world than Henry Fonda. If you took either of these two gentlemen and gave them a damn good series, they'd be successful. They say, "We have them, so who cares what it is!" That's not true at all. David Janssen was a big success in a series called "The Fugitive." David Janssen's new series wasn't a success. James Garner in his old series "Maverick" was a huge success. James Garner in his last western for Warner's was a disaster.

● *If David Janssen had not had a series such as "The Fugitive," do you believe he would have made it as a star?*
I don't know, but I think that some actors have what I call stardust. Some actors have it in varying degrees. I think you will agree with me that David has not made it as Paul Newman has made it. I remember using David Janssen on "Zane Grey Theatre." Previous to that I had never heard of him. In four years David did sixteen "Zane Grey Theatre"s and was marvelous. Every leading lady wanted to work with him. It was stardust. He wasn't Clark Gable, though he did two series and lots of pictures. I think there has to be something, and I think that thing is stardust.

● *Is it true that you found Michael Cole, who was one of the leads on "Mod Squad," in an actors workshop?*
Yes. Michael Cole studied with the Estelle Harmon Workshop. When she heard that we were doing "Mod Squad," she called and said she had a student named Michael Cole. Would I see him? I did. I think that's a responsibility of acting groups, to call a casting director if they have someone special. The college groups are so removed from Hollywood. At least at a place like Estelle Harmon's, she'll tell you some of the problems of the business. She'll tell you there are such things as cold readings, something most of these kids don't know about. When they come in, they do a scene from Shakespeare. Well, we don't do Shakespeare in television! Or they do a great scene from Molière. Well, you don't know if they can act or not.

● *Going back to Michael Cole. You met him in your office, on a recommendation of Estelle Harmon. Then what happened? Did you screen test him?*

Yes, we tested Michael and took a tremendous gamble. I thought Michael was a very good actor—had a marvelous look. He was perfect for the role but had terrible problems. He was taught stage acting at schools he'd gone to, and no one had told him that the camera is a huge monster and you have to act to those eyes, those windows. He was doing strange things with his hands; he was slumping—all the things the camera picks up— but Michael is bright and worked very hard. After four shows he was a motion picture actor.

● *Do you think that being in a series for a number of years will benefit him, or do you think he will be typecast?*

No. Since Michael did "Mod Squad" he did a "Movie of the Week" for me and he works steadily in television. Mine was a science-fiction picture, completely different from "Mod Squad," and in the other picture he played a paraplegic—completely different, too. We did a western series with a good young actor at Four Star, and that series lasted five years. That young actor went on to pictures and became a pretty big star—Steve McQueen. It didn't hurt him. We thought James Garner was going to be typed after "Maverick," but with *The Americanization of Emily* he started out on a very big career. Those days are really over. I think finally that we've stopped being the bastard child of motion pictures, and they're not holding it against us.

● *Is it easier for the young actor to break into television rather than feature films?*

It's easier in one sense because there's more TV—a lot more television. It's easier for me to gamble on an actor in a one-day part, because if it doesn't work, how much can it hurt me? If I'm doing a three-million-dollar picture, it could hurt me a great deal.

● *Is it better for an actor to take a part on TV than in one of those low-budget pictures?*

Much better. My nephew got a lead in one of those pictures, but no one's going to see it. It's almost as if he hadn't done it. One good TV show like a "Marcus Welby" show can do much more. TV film is the best film because of the time limitation. If you get a part—a quick, short scene—that's the kind of film you need, because no one's going to sit through a whole picture to see you in the last two minutes.

● *Do you think there are some actors who are exceedingly good in television but couldn't cut it in a motion picture?*

It works the other way. There are some marvelous motion picture actors and actresses that are terrible in television—so many close-ups; you see so much; you really can't fake television as you can motion pictures. The best actors for television are usually stage actors, because we have the time element, shooting maybe nine, ten, eleven pages a day.

● *Therefore, you feel you have to be a better actor for television than for feature film?*

Yes, I think so. I just don't think you get the help. You don't get Robert Wise or Peter Bogdanovich directing you. In television you get television directors. There are some very good television directors, but I think they'd be the first to admit they have such a time limit. Their job is to get it done. So a young actor or a new actor, they're just not getting the help that you would get in motion pictures where they rehearse for maybe three weeks and then shoot. The problem I'm interested in is what does an actor do to get to that stage? None of us three can help him once he's on the stage. Either he can act or he can't act, or he has a personality that the camera loves or he doesn't.

● *We have interviewed directors, all respected and well known. Each has said, "My door is open. I will see anyone." Do you believe this to be true?*

Not only don't I believe them, but I think it's misleading. Just let somebody call them and say, "I'm an actor and I'm in from Wisconsin and may I have an appointment?" See what your answer is. We do eleven "Movies of the Week," "The Rookies," pilots, and two features. I don't have the time. I think those people who you've mentioned, if they got their casting directors to see the actors, part of the problem would be solved. In the old days Warner Brothers saw new people—one hour every Monday. That doesn't exist anymore. The only way you're going to get into a studio now to see a casting director is when an agent makes an appointment. So we get back to the first step. How does an actor get an agent? I think the only way you can get an agent is to be with an acting group or get a part first. The most difficult thing in this town is getting an agent.

● *How do you feel about agents generally?*

Agents are marvelous when you come in and say, "I have Warren Beatty and he gets four hundred thousand dollars a picture. Would you like to handle him?" Writing agents are better, because writing agents at least must read the material. If they read a script that's written by an unknown writer and they're agents worth their salt, they say, "This is a good writer and I want to gamble with him." What does an actor do? All he can say is, "Will you come and see me in a play?" and the agent mostly says, "I'm too busy to do that." It's a horrible thing to say, but that's the bottleneck.

I remember years ago in pictures when [S. Z.] "Cuddles" Sakall always played the nice Jewish agent who loved his clients and was with them every day. That doesn't exist anymore. I was with an agency for fourteen years. My company and I grossed for them something like four and a half million dollars, and I didn't get a wedding present! On the other hand, Lee Marvin and Meyer Mishkin have had a marvelous relationship for over twenty years. That's a real love affair, but that's very rare as a rule.

● *If an agent doesn't get an actor work in the first few months, should the actor change agents?*

No; because if you're a beginning actor, you can thank your ass you have an agent and stay with him, be nice to him and, if you can, take him out to dinner and try to get to him. All an agent should do is to get you in to see an Aaron Spelling or a Bert Remsen. That's his job. An actor can't blame the agent. His job is only to get you interviews. Now, when you've gotten the part and you've some pretty good film and the agent is no longer moving with you, then my advice is to leave and go with another agent.

● *What about photographs?*

Unless you're a beautiful girl or a very attractive young man, photographs don't mean a damn thing. If you were to call me and say, "I'd like to send you a picture of a girl," and you sent me a picture of the most ravishing girl in the world—so ravishing that if I knew I could get her to say her name, we've got lightning in a bottle—I'd see her. Or if you sent me a picture of a young Tony Curtis, I would see him, because I'd say, "Wow, he'd be good in a series!" But send me a picture of anybody that is not ravishingly beautiful, and that picture goes in the wastebasket. Those composites showing one photo with a frown, the other with a scowl, and maybe one with a beard—it just doesn't work. They don't mean anything. If you have a sexpot girl, yes, because you can send that picture to an agent. She'll get a call. Now, she may get a call for the wrong reasons. She may get some agents who may try to lay her, but she's going to find some good agents who say, "What a striking face!"

● *Do you generally typecast a leading part?*

I would like to lie to you and say I see a lot of actors, that I don't typecast, but that would be a lie. When I'm looking for someone as a menace to David Janssen, and he's got to be a truck driver, I obviously want a big, burly truck driver. I would find it interesting if the driver had a beard, but I haven't seen a truck driver with a beard. They're usually such hardhats. That would be typecasting with style, but the chances are that when Bert Remsen, my casting director, suggests that so-and-so would be good, I can turn to the directory, see his picture, and say, "He looks interesting. Let's read him for it." I think one of the joys of being an actor is that now there are all sorts of TV movies. There are 103 TV movies on the air. Therefore, I do think there's an opportunity for new actors. In the picture we're doing with David Janssen, there was not one player outside of David Janssen, Keenan Wynn, Jeannette Nolan, and Tom Tully that I've ever seen. And I watch regular TV, so I know they're not just the stock performer, and we have twenty-three roles in this picture. I think the most important thing is to be yourself. I think what you want to get is a fresh look that's just in.

● *If your casting director interviews an actor and isn't impressed, couldn't it just be that you and he don't have the same taste? Perhaps if you saw him, you would hire him?*
That's true. On the other hand, the young writer doesn't get past my story editor. He can't come and see me. And if a director can't get by my producer, he can't come to see me either! Actually, there's not that much time in the day for a producer to see every actor and every writer and every director and every agent. I think if a casting director doesn't reflect the personality of the producer, either the producer is totally dumb or he's a very bad producer. I hope to God Bert Remsen, my casting man, is a reflection of me, because I would like to be a reflection of him. I think the man is a sensitive human being who cares, and I couldn't have anybody with me who was not that in the casting department. He was one of the few people who was a very successful actor. Unfortunately, he had a terrible accident and yet became a most successful casting director. The problem is that the producers and casting directors expect to get actors cheap, and that's one of their first mistakes. The picture-maker says, "All I want is to make pictures that must make a lot of money and not cost too much." That's what it's all about. That's the entertainment business. It's a devouring business. Hopefully there may be an hour or two of your time per month that you say, or you should say, "I'll interview young actors!"

# Daniel Mann
## Director

"There is nothing that I could have done that I don't feel
I could have done better."

Daniel Mann was born in New York City on August 8, 1912. He attended school at Erasmus Hall, Brooklyn, and the Professional Children's School. He began his career as a musician in resort hotels in both the United States and Canada. After having served in the U.S. Army during World War II, he received a scholarship to the Neighborhood Playhouse in New York, where he received his early training as a director.
His credits include:

Broadway Plays

*Come Back, Little Sheba*
*The Rose Tattoo*
*A Streetcar Named Desire*
*Paint Your Wagon*

Films

*Come Back, Little Sheba*
*About Mrs. Leslie*
*The Rose Tattoo*
*I'll Cry Tomorrow*
*The Teahouse of the August Moon*
*Hot Spell*
*The Last Angry Man*
*The Mountain Road*
*Butterfield 8*
*A Dream of Kings*
*For Love of Ivy*
*Willard*
*Maurie*
*Lost in the Stars*

Daniel Mann was editing his last picture, *Maurie,* and preparing the next, *Lost in the Stars,* when we met with him at his offices on the Twentieth Century-Fox lot. A delightful, gray-haired, goateed man in his early sixties, with a perennial suntan, the years seem to have slipped by him graciously, affecting him very little in looks, personality, and way of "up-to-date" thinking. We both felt this was due to his hard work in a creative career, which continues to turn over talented people like some high-powered piece of machinery. But in an industry where people seem to come and go so fast, Daniel Mann has managed to remain one of the few on top.

● *Do you find it imperative as a director to go with actors who have film or television experience? Or are you willing to give breaks to unknowns?*

It's never a question of simply giving them a break because I like someone in the office. If an actor or actress has the presence and the kind of impact I'm looking for, then I'll work with him, make a point to read with him, and have a chance to see how he responds to direction. I have to go on my own instincts and experience, and I've learned over the years always to make a comparison to music, so let me answer your question this way: If I were looking for the sound of brass, the greatest violinist in the world wouldn't do it for me. If I'm looking for a certain quality in terms of a personality or individual in a show, it is more important that the individual has that certain "it" that I'm looking for than credits or prestige. Now if I find someone who has both prestige and the quality, the exhibitor or financial people usually feel they have a certain amount of insurance, but even that's changing, because people don't go to a film to see personalities anymore. They go, I believe, to see *new* talent; that's the excitement.

May I say something about complete unknowns? The complete unknowns are those people, and I'm categorizing them for myself, who would have little or no experience. I'm not interested in an actor knowing his craft. I'm interested in an actor who has the presence when we work or when we talk of making me feel that he's just not someone with hair and teeth who's now decided to become an actor. An actor must have training and experience; and an actor, in this case, is sometimes known but not star known.

● *So, therefore, sometimes you feel it more valuable to go with a new actor than with a name?*

It depends on the film, and I try to be as pure—and I'm not talking about lily white—but I must say, that in some cases, the new actor really doesn't have the experience. There are many factors which are now stronger in my mind than they were, say, ten years ago. Pictures are being made for less money, and we really have to relate all our questions and answers to the circumstances, the whole cultural pattern in America. There *was* a time when it was possible to rehearse with young actors, but now, if an actor doesn't have experience, I don't have the time, with a tight budget, to teach him how to respond. Also, I want to direct a film and not coach actors!

● *Is it more difficult for you to direct the unknown actor?*

I don't think it's more difficult; I think it's different. And it depends very much on the production and the people involved. For example, I've just done this film with Bernie Casey, who's done a few films, and I think that Bernie is far ahead of the "stars" that I've worked with and that is a perfect example. I'd do a picture with him tomorrow.

● *How did you find Bernie Casey, for instance?*

The producer and writer, in preparation for this film *Maurie*, had evidently seen him or heard of him. On their suggestion I went to see a film that he had done, not a terribly good film, but he was effective. He had a quality that I liked. In this picture he plays out of his deepest sensitivity and awareness and is magnificent. I don't know whether he'd be able to get a starring role in another picture. It would have to be absolutely right for him.

● *Do you still make screen tests?*

I haven't made a screen test in years and years; it's too expensive with independent operations. But what I do do is this: Take, for instance, in this particular film that I'm doing now; there are a couple of people who I talked to, who I saw on film or other things that they did—totally unrelated to the role I was looking for—but I cast them because they were just right for the part.

● *Do you feel a director can cause a bad performance from an actor or actress who is usually extremely good at his or her craft?*

No question about it. Absolutely. And also vice versa, especially in films. Getting into this whole thing of directing, I feel that there are very good movie-makers and there are many good directors, and a good director should be a good movie-maker and a good movie-maker should be a good director. Many successful and important films have been made by great movie-makers who are not good directors. Many good directors have failed miserably in not making good pictures because they're not good movie-makers, because the art of direction—where the author ends and the actor begins, and where the actor ends and the director begins, and the director ends and the audience begins—is a chain of events building some kind of a marvelous statue. And the full contribution of each of those individuals is not merely a question of how good they are but how full they are based on selectivity, based on the atmosphere in which they worked, based on the amount of money which has been allowed for rehearsal and production values, based on a kind of marvelous personalized impulse which comes with talent but also in a work atmosphere where that's possible. That does not always happen.

I've worked with young actors such as Marisa Pavan, Terry Moore, people like that who had Academy Award nominations in *Sheba* and *Tattoo*. I haven't heard of them since. Now this doesn't mean that I'm a Svengali, but this means that I demanded from them and they were able to give for that role the kind of personalized things that other people hadn't asked for. I used to believe years ago I could get a performance from anybody—that was an ego thing. I find now I'm much more interested to work with actors who bring me something that I can work with in their presence, in their attitude, rather than saying, "Well, I'll have to pull it out." A lot depends on the material, a lot on the actor, his power and concentration. But more importantly, there is nothing that I have done that I don't feel I could have done better, and I think actors feel the same way, but they're not always given a second chance.

There are many accidents in art, but I do think that casting is very important in film. An individual cast properly would do much better in the role—again the example of music—the greatest trumpet in the world is not going to do for the sound of a fiddle.

● *Thinking in terms of yourself, do you feel it important that an actor be intelligent, that he or she be able to communicate with you on a certain level and have a good personality on a first interview?*

Personality is a very important element, because it's the presence of those individuals that I will be communicating with—their senses, their selectivity, their approach—and much of that they're born with and then it's developed in an environment, in a society that allows that person to develop. But that really has nothing to with talent. Talent, as I define it, is the ability to overcome your problems. That's all I can describe talent as. For example, I've never worked with a genius. Everyone I know had to work very hard to achieve the fullest expression, the statement that they wanted to make in their work.

Of all the people I've ever worked with, I'd say Anna Magnani is the most natural, because her senses and her instrument are so finely, sensitively tuned that her emotional vigor is something that can be called on—not displayed, but used—very personally. And yet I don't think of Anna as an intellectual. This doesn't mean that she's not without knowledge. She's worldly; she's a great combination of many things—mature, immature, childlike, passionate, wildly expressive in all of her manners and her antics—and yet in her life this woman has had many problems and much sadness. So it's very difficult for me to answer your question about personality. Personality is charisma, charm— and that's important because the camera will see that and magnify it.

● *What we are trying to say is this: possibly that's a way through the door, the first step in the right direction. Because if you're bad on an interview and the person who is interviewing you doesn't know your work, it can be a terrible barrier. But if you're relaxed, at ease, and have something to say, it's got to be helpful.*

Yes, it is important. But you see, being at ease can be a phony act. Coming on too strong and being a personality can be very, very bad in terms of alienating someone like myself. What I really look for in a person is what I call their own sense of object—their ability to sit, be relaxed, and talk to me on their level. I'm not

125

judging them, but I want to bring them out. With some people, sitting across a desk can make them very shy. Then it's up to me to reach that individual by being direct and very honest. But there are no shortcuts. You've got to be yourself. Many people think when they come into an office the whole emphasis is on being "with it," whatever that is. The guys come in with their shirts open to their navel; the women come in with great décolletage—who challenge me as they sit across the table. That's so wrong for a guy like me. That's an aspect I may be interested in as a role, but the greater goal is total personality and not merely that one manifestation.

● *What about the actor or actress who is very definitely a type?*

They have a tough time, because there are conventions in this country which are reflections of our whole cultural pattern. You can say this person is a character and this person is a leading man or lady, but usually I have found that character actors are people who have to work harder because they don't have the other attributes. I find them very interesting and extremely important and different.

● *Have you ever worked with an actor who was a great stage actor and didn't succeed on film?*

No. I find that some of the fantastic stage actors who were very conscious of their voice and very conscious of a kind of projection—that that was a limitation on the stage as well. Whereas the theater is the art of the spoken word, motion pictures is the art of the spoken word and the actor's impulse. I've often said that music is the sound of life, and painting is the line and color of life, and acting must be the impulse of life, and that impulse has to be evoked spontaneously. Many actors in the theater have that, but they push it beyond what is necessary in order to make it bigger. But in films it's a very simple technique. Acting is acting in any form—television or theater. The fact that there's a camera or you sit in a comfortable chair in an auditorium with thousands of watts of light to project the impulses—magnify it a thousand times—means that the actor's reality—the camera—will project it; the sound will project it. In stage acting it's behavior, and so it is in motion pictures.

● *Do you feel actors should work in plays?*

I think that unless an actor acts he's not an actor. Any experience he gets, even bad experience, can be turned into something beneficial. I find myself, when I cast a picture, trying to get around to see some of the plays. I try also to think of some of the young people I've seen, who I know, et cetera.

● *What is your feeling about a screen personality such as Clint Eastwood or John Wayne who probably would never have made it via the stage?*

Well, I don't know too much about Mr. Eastwood except that he's enormously successful and I've seen some of his pictures. It's completely different. In films there is a marketable place for stars as such, but in theater it's different—the whole economics, the kind of limitation, that plays aren't being written and there's a tradition. So for Mr. Eastwood—most of whose successes have been in westerns and who's a popular figure—he achieves a certain kind of reality that's necessary for that kind of picture. I certainly wouldn't compare his success with the kind of training and discipline and years of work that one achieves in theater. But there is no theater for young people—a little, but certainly not enough to give us a new generation of actors.

I'm of the mind that there are many people who are programmed to be successful, and their success as the final goal is to be rich and famous in the ways you can become rich and famous, to be enriched by a life of dedication to your craft, the world you live in, to some way nourish yourself. And I use the word *nourish*. In this country we don't have a national theater, and when you talk about craft there's so much craft that's not craft, so many schools of acting that have taken away some bad habits of Broadway but replaced them with bad habits of a certain school. And the actor must find himself, and the actor must develop the ability to be courageous, make mistakes, work. That's why I think any place they can do that is important; even if it's a bad place, they must begin an arena of activity.

● *Do you think a young actor who is just beginning to find himself and who obtains a part on a television series can be hurt if the character he portrays is a banal one and he's locked into that role for several years?*

If playing a banal character for three or four years is the only way you can get experience, do it. When you think, for example, that Picasso had a style of painting which changed as he developed, as he wanted to extend his horizon, there is no reason why an actor should be ruined if he or she can maintain a standard and, at the same time, develop some kind of studio activity where he is making a living at acting and where he is also developing aspects he can use. You don't just sit home and wait for the perfect play, just like you don't sit home and wait for the perfect world. You've got to live in it and make it that way.

● *Do you use a casting director?*

I use a casting director because he or she will bring me
people that I don't know. There are some young people
that they have seen because that's their business, and I
use the Player's Directory mostly as a reference. I'm
always happy to meet someone I don't know. If
anybody tells me there's a young man or young woman
who's talented and I should see them, I'm anxious to,
because it could be the discovery of someone very
important. I've had some great and unusual things
happen. I did a picture a long time ago called *The Last
Angry Man*. In that picture I cast three young actors.
One was Cicely Tyson; one was Godfrey Cambridge;
and the other was Billy Dee Williams. These were three
young people who I saw in New York while casting and
gave them small parts. I realized when Cicely made this
marvelous impression with her role in *Sounder* that
this was the same girl I had worked with years ago, and
she was great then. She did a marvelous job. I think that
most people don't realize that these actors have been
around, and working hard, for years. Like Gene
Hackman. We did that picture with Cicely I think in
the late fifties, early sixties, and she's been working
hard all these years at her craft and holding her breath
when she couldn't work.

● *Does the black actor still have a problem being typed?*

Depends on the pictures. I'm very happy to feel that
there are many more opportunities now for black
actors—like in the last couple of pictures I've done and
the one I'm doing now—but I think all things that
apply to actors apply to actors black or white. There are
those exploitation pictures, using the black scene for
just the same reason as the producer uses the
pornographic scene. There is no reason a black actor is

not capable of playing any kind of a role—roles about people, black or white. I would like to see the day when there can be mixed casts, doing the classics or any contemporary play. I did a picture, *For the Love of Ivy,* with Sidney Poitier and Abbey Lincoln. They were *people,* and the picture was successful. It was accepted by both black and white.

● *Do you believe that photos are vitally important to the actor?*

Only for a form of record. When I interview someone, I say "Do you have a picture?"—not because I'm interested to see how they photograph, but if I've seen fifty or seventy people I want to be able to have a clear mind—one good picture that is a natural shot. The actress or actor should not be allowed to create an image *they* think they look like. In other words, be courageous; be individual; be yourself.

● *Is it still possible for a young, attractive actress to get there by way of the casting couch?*

Yes, because I think the woods are full of people who are still conditioned by the sex drive, and lots of people have their own personal needs. Look what's happening with the kind of pornographic films—one or two particularly that are making millions. It depends on what you're interested in.

● *Who is one of the most exciting young performers you've seen in recent years?*

Al Pacino has an unusual quality. I've never worked with him, but I feel he has a kind of inner life that creates a kind of reality in the sense that he plays fully and has an instrument that's attuned in some way to the art of acting. I don't know his growth, his development, but I think that's an unusual talent. I think Bernie

Casey—the man I just did this film with—is another
outstanding actor. He epitomizes what I think an actor
should have—talent, intelligence, and selectivity that
comes out of knowing where you are in the world and a
constant involvement *with* the world. That makes
talent today, and actors have to have this. It's important
for actors to be aware, to know who they are as human
beings, to be aware of what is going on, keeping up
with the world issues, et cetera, other than thinking in
terms of just themselves. All those aspects of life will be
the things they are going to express. And when they are
in some way in tune with all the forces—social,
economic, psychological, philosophical—it will give
them a greater range in their acting. It's not enough to
be a good actor without knowing what you act. What
do you act? You act and express your own personal
statement, and unless acting is personal it's never right.

I think Anna Magnani was the most exciting
actress I have ever worked with, the most instinctive.
I've worked with many exciting actresses, actresses who
have had exciting moments. Magnani, in *Rose Tattoo,*
which was a marvelous role for her, played out of a deep
inner life in that particular role and also in everything
she does. I've seen her in other things where I didn't feel
she was as effective. The role is so very important to the
actress, too. But I wouldn't say that Magnani is way,
way above everybody else. I've worked with other
marvelous people—Shirley Booth, Susan Hayward—
people who have had great moments and great scenes
and great ability. I believe that an actor is limited by his
role and by the director that he works with.

# Telly Savalas

## Actor

"How would you feel being in lollipop land
blowing up balloons—all the time?"

Telly Savalas was born in Garden City, New York. He attended Holy Cross Institute in Connecticut and Long Island's Sewanhaka High School, interrupting his education to enlist in the army at the outbreak of World War II. After three years of service, he resumed his schooling and graduated with a B.S. degree from Columbia University. He then joined the Information Service of the State Department and later moved to ABC as a senior director of news and special events. He created the "Your Voice of America" series, which won him both a Freedom Foundation and a Peabody Award. His acting career earned him an Academy Award nomination as best supporting actor in 1962 for *Birdman of Alcatraz*. Since then he has won the Emmy Award for lead actor in a dramatic series for his performance as Kojak.

Films

*The Young Savages*
*The Greatest Story Ever Told*
*Cape Fear*
*Beau Geste*
*The Man from the Diner's Club*
*The Dirty Dozen*
*Buona Sera, Mrs. Campbell*
*Crooks and Coronets*
*Kelly's Heroes*
*In Her Majesty's Secret Service*

Motion Pictures for Television

*Mongo's Back in Town*
*Visions*
*The Marcus-Nelson Murders*

We met with Telly Savalas in his trailer at Universal Studios, where he was shooting a segment of his popular series, "Kojak." He was wearing a suit and tie, and his face was thick with make-up. While we interviewed him between takes, his entourage, including his brother, George, and friends from "long ago," kept floating in and out the door. Telly Savalas of the ever-alert, blue-blue eyes was a hard interview—hard because one doesn't know where the actor leaves off and the person begins. And is there any end or any beginning? Perhaps not. Happy with life, thrilled with his present success, he gives the impression of wanting more, much more, and of wanting people to know him—not as a superstar on television but as the person he really is. The big question is, "Who is that person?"

● *You are quite extraordinary in that you've been in this business a long time—*
   Not true. I'm a Johnny-come-lately.
● *Well, you didn't come lately.*
   That's true. And now that I think about it, a dozen years is a long time.
● *Can you tell us briefly how you started out as an actor?*
   Well, I've told the story so many times, in the retelling I tend to change it a little bit each time so as not to bore myself. I find it terribly disillusioning to watch performers doing the same thing all the time. For me, a necessary prerequisite is to be entertaining to myself. If I find myself getting commercial or duplicative, I get upset. I haven't thought of a new version yet, but if it should happen spontaneously within the course of this interview, I'll tell the story again.
   I didn't start out to be an actor. It happened by chance. I was an executive with the State Department, and one day I got a call from a theatrical agent asking if I knew someone to play a part of an old European judge in a television show. I knew just the man, but I couldn't get in touch with him. So *I* went to the audition in order to satisfy protocol and diplomacy. Besides, nobody would know who it was but me. I went in with my phony accent and read, strictly for a gag. They said I was a little young for the part, but would I do it? I told them I'd call them tomorrow. It was shocking.
   I went to see my mother. "Ma," I said, "they want me to do this television show and they will pay me three hundred dollars. What do you think?" "Telly," she said, "you do it. You'll be a glorious actor."
   I did it, and from that day to this I've never looked back. There are many losses and many rewards in an acting career, but it must not be looked at as the

pinnacle of success but merely as a gay wave going along the shores. And I'm riding that wave. If it subsides, as it one day will, I'll get on to more important things.

● *Do you feel you've reached the ultimate as an actor?*

Good Lord, no—the bottom of the barrel. They've yet to realize that I'm a sixteen-year-old Romeo looking to get out—forget that I look like a gorilla—do you understand? The challenges to date have been minimal, and I'm still waiting for that maximum challenge. Then I will both satisfy myself and I think satisfy the audience when they realize finally who Telly is. I'm in a cookie cutter here. "Kojak," or whatever you think of as a maximum success, to me is just a minimal part of who I am as an extrovert and do as an elastic type of performer.

● *When you decided to be an actor, did you then start to study?*

No; I never made that concession to myself that I was going to be an actor. As I've said, it happened quite by accident, and when they asked me to do it again—still for money—well, I couldn't believe that these wonderful things were happening—that they were paying me a great deal of money for something I had been doing all my life for free.

● *What do you think has made you the great success that you are today? If you were to look at yourself, what would you see? In other words, why are you the top TV star today?*

You notice I didn't interrupt you when you were saying those wonderful things. But if we're going to be honest and analytical as regards commercial success—which in the end result is very important—I would credit it to my ordinariness, the fact that people all over the world can identify with me and say, "Telly Savalas, you gorilla, you're just like I am and you made it." And people are cheering. That's it.

● *What about your sex appeal?*

I'm not what you call a butterfly, and where romance has taken place with me, it's been on a one-on-one basis. It's always building memories in a quiet corner.

● *Let's put it this way—do you think your career would have gone differently if you had not been so unusual to look at?*

Well, your choice of words is unfortunate. My mother would have replaced the word *unusual* with *classic*. My mother says that I've been beautiful for three thousand years, and if you don't believe it, go look at the statues on Mount Olympus. Go look at the Parthenon. "Telly," my mother said, "your kind of chiseled head has been beautiful since the dawn of civilization." I have no reason to argue with my mother. Hollywood has not seen this. They've given me a gun, a bomb, and said, "Here, act." They should have given me a girl in the beginning and said, "Telly is pretty. Let him be pretty with the opposite sex." I was born to be romantic.

● *But don't you think that's part of your sex appeal—that it's not just a person's looks but an energy that comes from inside?*

Well, if I were going to define sex appeal, I would define it with traits which are mine—softness, sentimentality, companionship, affection. If that's sex appeal, then that, of course, adds up to Telly. If you correlate sex appeal with the things I've mentioned, fine. I'm not Casanova and I resent the image. I resent the impression given that I would haphazardly seduce with my personality. I love, and there's a difference between loving and getting laid. I'm glad I said that!

139

● *Getting back to your beginning as an actor, once you'd made up your mind to commit yourself to acting as a profession, did you then get an agent? What did you do?*

Well, we speak about the responsibilities of performance, and I must confess that from one day when you wanted your mother's attention and you cried a little bit louder for your bottle of milk or because your diapers were wet, performances begin, and I must admit that from the beginning I was pretty good. When the gas man came to the door and my mother was hiding in the closet, I had to get rid of him, telling him that Mama wasn't home. Performances begin. I reached a mature stage in my life when somebody started paying me to perform, and to this day I'm astonished. It's just now that I'm beginning to be comfortable as a performer—a commercial performer.

● *Well, you're a natural born actor.*

We all are. I have only one talent, my ability to be myself when the red light goes on or when the curtain goes up. But we're all performers.

● *True, but all of us can't let go, and that's why everybody isn't an actor.*

That's a psychological adjustment, and I know I have the ability to pass this adjustment on to others—you know, the ability to be themselves—and one day I'll do just that.

● *Do you ever want to play a character different from yourself?*

Aspects of myself and my experience. I'm going to play somebody that's believable in the commercial world. It's not little theater! Luckily for them and for me, they're beginning to see me in other dimensions. If you miss the spirit of me, if you suggest that it's arrogance or egotistical, you miss the interview. You do know

that? Don't paint me as a tiger; I'm a pussycat. That's
the truth, but because I speak quickly and spontaneously and honestly, so many times it can be mistaken for
arrogance. And that's not my nature; I cry very easily.

If you're going to measure it from my commercial
success, you have to listen to what I have to say, right?
Now, from my shallow experience, let's blow the
whistle on the world. Of course, you do have to be
concerned with the mechanics of speech, accents and
things like that, but they're the mechanics of acting. If
I'm going to advise young actors, I would say the one
thing they have going for themselves is their own
uniqueness. If we believe in the uniqueness of the
individual—and I've been taught that way, that every
person is different—well, hold on to that difference;
make it grow. What does it all mean—uniqueness?
Well, I cry a certain way and I laugh a certain way. No
one is going to teach me that. So what is my
responsibility if I want to be an actor, an intelligent
extrovert? That's my responsibility, to be just that—
myself. More advice—get up in front of people. Do
things. Fancy yourself a prince when you order a cup of
coffee at the local diner. Play parts every day—and you
don't need a stage for that—and then, when your
moment comes, you're ready. In fact, it's easier. Some
other slob is going to give you words. You don't have to
ad-lib. Experience, right out into the field. If you have
youth and beauty for sale, don't dissipate it wasting
years in drama schools. Get out into the field. Go do it!
The heartbreaks are there, so protect yourself as well,
because it's a very dangerous profession. It's not like
selling brushes. As the Fuller Brush man, if they close
the door in your face, you can say to yourself, "They
don't like my brushes." When you go for a job as an

actor, they're closing the door on *you*. They're saying *no* to *you*, and that can damage your ego. Ninety percent of talent, I feel, is confidence. Lose that confidence, and you lose your spirit. That's dangerous, so try to protect that. You can protect that by knowing that these disappointments are coming and by getting someone who has faith in your talent and acts as your agent and does all the liaison work. That way you protect yourself. Then if you're destined to be a performer, it will happen. One day it will happen.

● *Then it's really a matter of perseverance?*
Yes, but in the face of failure when they say, "Hmm, you're bald," or "Gee, your nose is too big," you have to know how to adjust to those things.

● *Does luck play any part in it?*
You want me to answer honestly? Luck plays a part in everything. I'm on a merry-go-round, and I don't want to get off because I'm lazy and they're paying me twice as much in a week as I used to make in a year as a dedicated, important employee.

● *Aren't you happier now than you were then?*
How would you feel being in lollipop land blowing up balloons—all the time?

● *Don't you enjoy acting?*
I love it. I love it, but it has its disadvantages as well.

● *Doesn't every business? How do you feel about going on from acting—to writing or directing?*
I've done all that. I took eight days off a while back and wrote a screenplay. I wrote a brilliant screenplay, and I've already directed. I've sold the screenplay to a major studio, and I'm going to make a picture—as the producer, director, star, and writer. Wow, I haven't written the music yet! And, I've made an album—I'm singing songs!

● *So your point of view is that the young actor doesn't need to sharpen his tools by learning how to act?*

Just hold on to your uniqueness. There's no need to pose, to walk like Marilyn Monroe. Maybe Jane Smith is cuter. A good actor is someone that can emulate life within his own personality and convince people that he is real.

● *Did you ever have bad times as an actor?*

As an actor, none, but smart enough, I think, to realize what the sad times would be. But, affection being one of my prerequisites for life and living, and one of the benefits of being a "star" is to surround yourself with your own people—that's what it's about. What a tragic day it would be if I enjoyed this kind of notoriety and success and I didn't have the people who loved me around me—people who can relate to it and be excited by it. What a terrible world that would be. I've always loved people—had a passion for them. Now in my first picture I was nominated for an Academy Award. I didn't know what was going on, but it was all very lovely and exciting. I thank God for my maturity, because this kind of success can blow you totally out of proportion—people coming over and saying, "Gee, you're wonderful." And you say, "Wasn't I wonderful before?" That's an adjustment. Success too can be dangerous—not only failure.

● *Perhaps this love of life and of people, an awareness of persons and things around you, has helped you be a good actor.*

I've given no thought in that direction.

● *As an actor, how do you approach a part? Are there parts you don't want to play?*

I don't shun any parts. If I'm playing a villain, I make sure he's a villain. My responsibility as a human being

is to make him as unattractive as possible. I hate villains
as heroes—hate heroes as heroes—hate anybody that's
capable of killing another person or hurting them. And
if they want me to paint him in a glorious light, I'll
have nothing to do with it. For example, the part I
played in *The Dirty Dozen* was a completely despicable
character. I made sure I showed the paranoia, the
schizophrenia behind the personality. And when I play
a good guy, as in "Kojak," you will see that he rarely
takes out his gun—unless, of course, he's up against the
wall—but for the most part he tries to use intelligence,
tries to use diplomacy. I don't like violence of any kind,
so I never play anything dealing with violence in any
attractive way.

● *What has been the most exciting part you have played?*
The most involving was as Pontius Pilate in *The
Greatest Story Ever Told,* directed by George Stevens.
In that I became thoroughly involved—I really thought
I was Pontius Pilate—not because of me, but because of
the grand performance of Max Von Sydow as Christ.

● *Does the director that you're working with play an
important part for you as an actor?*
Yes, more often than not a director will have an insight
that perhaps has eluded me.

● *You've worked in both feature films and television. Where
would you rather be?*
It makes no difference. The power of television is tremendous. I've made over sixty very important films with
the great stars of the world, and two major shots on television have given me more recognition than all of those
films put together. When you're reaching sixty, seventy,
and eighty million people a night, it's a little scary. It's
satisfying for me in television; we're the number-one
show. But, of course, I'll get back to features.

●*How do you cope with success in relation to your private life?*

Well, for a man who has affectionately pursued people all my life, now they've made my job easier—they pursue me. From that point of view, I have no regrets at all. Regrets come in other areas. I never know if they want to meet Telly or Telly the Movie Star, and that's a loss.

● *Aren't you one and the same person really?*

Yes, but who's going to take the time to discover it? People are in awe because they see me on the screen or in television. I'd like to tell them that in me there's an ordinariness, there's a niceness they might like if they ever got to know me.

● *But one does change with success, and you're no longer ordinary.*

I disagree. I look at my ordinariness with a great deal of pride. Now if you're saying does my personality change?—well, one thing I've always thought of as an important quality is my consistency as a human being. Success or failure will do nothing to change that. My father taught me that at a very young age.

● *Yes, but there's a growth that is change.*

Growth in what way? Growth whereby egoism will give place to compassion? Never. If I begin to think I'm as wonderful as people think I am for doing something which I don't thoroughly understand, then I'm in a lot of trouble.

● *Isn't it a matter of whether one likes oneself or not?*

I adore myself, but that doesn't mean I know myself. As Socrates, that great Greek philosopher, said, "Know thyself." I haven't quite discovered me yet. I'm still searching.

# Renee Valente

## Casting Director

"Tremendous sex appeal. That's what I think makes a star."

An attractive woman with a strong personality, Renee Valente wields a lot of power in Hollywood as vice president of Women in Film, an organization dedicated to helping women in the film industry. One gets the impression that, at this point in her successful career, the most exciting area for her is the battle for the new, unknown actor—a battle to be fought with producers, directors, and the networks. But, as she herself says with a smile, "You win some; you lose some." We are inclined to believe she wins more than she loses.

Renee Valente, Vice President of Talent for Screen Gems, is in charge of all casting for that studio. Her Screen Gems tenure began in 1964, when she entered the organization as a producer and assistant to the president of the International Division. Later, she was East Coast director of program projects and producer of the "Hawk" series starring Burt Reynolds. Prior to her association with Screen Gems, Renee Valente was with Talent Associates for more than a decade, functioning variously as an associate producer, production manager, and, ultimately, head of production. She worked in television (live tape and film), motion pictures, and the theater, and her credits include such notable productions for those media as "Play of the Week," "Edge of the City," "Rashoman," "Kraft Theatre," "Mr. Peepers," and "The Art Carney Special," for which she received an Emmy Award.

● *How did you become a casting director? What kind of background did you have?*

I started as a part-time typist with David Susskind's, Talent Associates. I'd left a job where I was paid a lot more money, and I figured that if I had anything on the ball, how long could I be kept as a part-time typist? That lasted for two weeks before I became a full-time secretary, and it wasn't long before I became budget controller, then head of production, producing shows with Susskind. I got into casting when I joined Screen Gems as the East Coast arm of development, and that of necessity brought me into dealing with the actor. I decided that if I were doing that I'd better get to know actors, so I called every agent in New York and said I wanted to see all their people. It took about eight months. Every day from nine to six I saw actors every ten minutes, not knowing that I would eventually be going into casting. I then became producer of "Hawk," a TV show starring Burt Reynolds. When that went on its rump, there was no job for me in New York, and Jackie Cooper, head of Screen Gems, asked me to come out to the West Coast and head up their casting department. I told him I didn't know if I could do that. I didn't know if I was equipped. But all those years behind me apparently gave me more equipment than I realized. I think it's necessary and vital to have that whole production background.

● *Have you ever found an actor that you wanted to gamble on, that you knew could be a star, and yet been unable to convince the people up above to use him?*

All the time. I went through it with Anthony Hopkins on the TV film *QB VII*—one of the times I've won the battle. Interestingly enough, a lot of top stars turned the role down. I found Hopkins in London. He cut short

151

his honeymoon and came in from Wales on a Saturday afternoon to meet with me in London and asked me to see a test he'd done for a film called *The Abdication.* I did and loved him. He's an amazing actor of thirty-two, and nobody knew him in this country. I went on to fight for him.

● *Who was it you had to fight—the producer?*

I had to fight everyone—my company, my producer, the network. Now they're thrilled. In their wildest dreams they never thought that this young actor would be so brilliant. I win more than I lose, and that's why I keep punching. When I produced "Hawk," I won the battle of putting Burt Reynolds in it. Nobody wanted him. Then, after the first year when the show was canceled, I wanted to put Burt in a comedy, and everybody thought I was absolutely insane. I knew his wit, his humor, but I couldn't do it. That's one I lost. As I said, you win some and you lose some.

● *When you were in England casting on* QB VII, *you had an opportunity to look at a lot of English actors. Are they superior in their profession?*

I don't like the word *superior.* They have an entirely different thrust to the business. In London they're not paid much money for their work so that beyond their training, even when they're in the theater, they are working for their craft to better themselves as actors. Too many American actors will turn down something because of money, where the British actor is far more dedicated to his craft than our American actors are. But that is the way they live there. I mean they have a very hard, rigid working system, and it's not that they're better, because we have unbelievably fine actors here. The trouble is that nobody goes to the ACT Company in San Francisco to see the brilliant work of Peter Donat and the other actors or the ACT in San Diego or all over this country. In London, as it is in New York, you're surrounded by theater and you can see so many actors, because it's all in a very small area. The English actors' dedication is on a different scale. It's not that they like money any less, but they have been trained all their lives in the acting field, and that becomes the prime factor rather than the dollars. You see, also in England, they're acclaimed royally, so that's something for them to look forward to. In this country, we don't have that.

● *In the seven years you've been casting for Screen Gems, have there been any radical changes for the actor?*

It's much harder for the young actor today. Five years ago anybody new would have had a great shot at it. Nobody wanted any big names then because of the new films and the new TV shows with all new people. It became very exciting. Today, we're almost going back to the old thinking of "It's got to be somebody that the TV audience knows because they can relate to him." It is very rare today that a new actor will get the shot he could have got five years ago. Five years ago there was an upheaval with the young people of the country, and so anything that was young and different was going to be exciting and was going to work. What television found was that the young people the shows were geared for were not at home watching and that the people who were at home watching the TV had a fear of these bearded, new-look, new-thinking young people.

● *What about feature films as opposed to television. Does the same thing apply?*

I think it does—*Easy Rider, Joe, Strawberry Statement,* the various and sundry films that were made for youth audiences. You notice today that we're going for more nostalgia. I think the backlash I talked about was because of what's happened in this country today, and nobody really knows why. It was bound to happen. A country can't be two hundred years old without strides being made and changes in so many things. I think what happened is that the strides that were taken happened so fast it scared a lot of people. What they want now is to go back to the kind of music that is warm and lovely and peaceful. The same thing applies in film and television. That's my theory.

● *So the chances of an unknown actor making it today are really slim. Is that due to the fact that a lot of top talent is going begging or that the networks are afraid to gamble?*

You used the right word—*gamble*. Because of the economy in our business today, more people are afraid to gamble, and that's because they have a great deal more to lose than they did years ago. In the early days if you made a mistake and something didn't work, the attitude was, "OK, so what's one picture going down the drain?" But today every picture is a live or die kind of thing and you've got to try and make money. Producers tend to feel they're going to make money if they've got a Steve McQueen in their film. In my opinion, this is not the way it should go, because the success—the real success—is that great new personality that people are going to latch onto and the excitement of it.

● *Very broadly, what do you think of actors? Do you find they have very short memories about the people who helped them get started?*

Good question, because "Hawk" was several years ago, and if you look at that plaque on the wall, it reads, "To

Renee Valente with sincere thanks for discovering this Indian, love and appreciation from Burt Reynolds, Xmas 1972." He hasn't forgotten, but that's a rare case.
● *What was the special quality Burt has that made you want him for "Hawk"? Was it his personality? A certain look? What?*

Tremendous sex appeal. That's what I think makes a star. If they don't have that appeal, no matter what tools they have, they might never become stars. They may be working actors all the time and may do very well, but I think *star* is a very special word. A star needs that appeal, and he sure has it. It's interesting that that's what it all boils down to.
● *Have you ever met an actor or an actress that you didn't like but that you still felt had that quality?*

Yes. In casting you have to separate yourself and you've got to be totally objective; otherwise you've lost it. I mean you must take yourself outside of yourself and look at actors like paintings. Although I may not care for Matisse, I can appreciate the beauty of what he does as a painter, and I think that's true also of actors.
● *Do you find that young male actors try to wine and dine you to get parts?*

Yes, but it doesn't apply just to the young males; even actresses do it. But I'm not easy to wine and dine. I was, the first year I came to California and thought everybody loved me for me, but I have since found out that those who love me for me will remain there no matter what happens. But I do appreciate their having to do it and feel the more you get to know somebody, the easier it is. I hold no ill feelings that they do it, because if I were an actor, I'd try everything also. When I meet an actor, I don't talk about his acting right away. I find that the last way to learn about him. I talk to him about motorcycles or sex or anything in the world to get him outside of himself.

● *When you interview an unknown actor, do you then take a photograph and résumé and file them away, or—*

Let me interrupt. When I don't know the actor's ability and I see something there that's interesting, I ask him to come back and do a scene or I ask if he's going to be in a play or if there's a piece of film I can see on him. I cannot call an actor in cold to read for a specific show, because the director and the producer don't want to see people that I or one of my casting directors haven't seen work. If they fall on their faces during the reading it's OK so long as we've seen them and know something about them.

● *When actors come into your office to do a scene for you, what specifics do you look for?*

I look for the actors relating to each other. I look for their sustaining character. I look for credibility in the scene and within that the personality and the feeling I get.

● *Does the director usually come to you and specifically request certain actors, or does he leave it mostly up to you to pick or suggest the actors?*

I'm very fortunate. I don't know how it happened, but I think that people have a lot of respect for my opinion. They know how I like to work, that I like to bring them people they have not necessarily worked with so that we do try new actors, and that's terribly important and that does work. Certainly, once in a while a director or a producer will say, "I think so-and-so would be great for that role," and I'd say, "I agree with you, but will you let me show you someone else, because you've used so-and-so time and time again. She's a working actress.

She makes a lot of money, and she's constantly seen. Just let me show you someone else."

● *What do you think could be done to help the unknown actor? Aaron Spelling suggested having one day a month on a sound stage when all the casting directors could come and watch new talent.*

I did something like that in New York for six years which I think was fantastic. I had a showcase once a month which lasted two hours—from six to eight P.M. so people could get home early. We had all new actors, new directors, new lighting directors and art directors. It was really a package of all new talent, and we did this through the Academy of Television Arts and Sciences. When I moved to California, one of the first calls I made was to the TV Academy here in Hollywood. They couldn't have been less interested. I think that what we did to showcase new talent in every area is what's needed. Now that takes a lot of time, but it's worth it, and in the long run it saves a lot of time. We used to have an audience of close to four hundred people a month, which included directors, casting directors, producers, et cetera. Now that means that all those new people were seen, and it gives the actor a great deal of hope, because you can't get a lot of people in this town to go to little theater.

● *Let's talk about agents. Isn't getting an agent one of the biggest problems an unknown actor faces?*

Yes, because agents today can no longer afford to take a lot of chances. It costs them money to handle people— money and time.

● *If an agent is not respected in the industry, can that stop the chances of an actor to work?*

Absolutely. Even the big agents can be harmful. I'll give you an example. A young, talented man came to our attention. We wanted to do something with him in one of our series, and nobody knew this young actor. He had signed with a heavyweight agent, and they did not want him to go into a series. Now I tell you that exposure on a TV series will do more for that young man than anything else, but they want to groom him, hopefully for variety shows and various other things. But in my opinion, one season on a series would do more for him. He's a very young boy, just eighteen, and he said to me, "I'm very disappointed, but I've got to put my career in their hands. God willing they're right."

● *Isn't it very often true that an actor who does get a role in a series becomes typecast so no one can see him in any other kind of part?*

That's very often true to a degree in both series and features. Burt Reynolds was typecast for fifteen years and finally broke the mold, as did Carroll O'Connor and Ed Asner—also after fifteen to twenty years.

● *Many times actors complain that casting directors don't have enough imagination or insight to see them in other roles than what they've seen them play before. Do you think that's true or not? Would it help if on an interview the actor went dressed for the part?*

That's an interesting question that's asked very often. In my opinion, an actor should go dressed for the role if he can. If I want a cowboy and the actor walks in with a suit and tie, I think that can be a hindrance. I think it's easier on the other hand for actresses, because women wear different clothes, can model themselves to what they want. But with men, it seems to make a difference.

● *What are the chances today for the young actress in her thirties?*

It is much more difficult for a woman. There are not as

many parts written for a woman as there are for men. Also, most of the parts arc for young women under thirty. When an actress gets over thirty, she's up against all those actresses that have a lot of years and experiences behind them. As an actress, Dyan Cannon got a great break because she was married to Cary Grant. That's what really brought her into promi- nence. I don't know whether she would have made it had she been married to Joe Smith.

● *What are your feelings about publicity?*

It's unbelievably important. Regarding publicity, Truman Capote once said that one should take two days of solid publicity and forget about the little dribbles, and he was absolutely right. Saturation campaign.

● *Some of the new generation of actors are turning away from publicity. Can't that be harmful?*

I think they're turning away from the fan magazines, because they exaggerate and lie so much. That's what they're turning their noses down at. I don't think they're turning their noses down at a line which says, "So-and-so is starring in a film," or "So-and-so was at the Ahmanson Theatre last night," or anything like that. I don't think they are against the right kind of publicity. I agree with them and don't think it's anybody's business who they're going to bed with, but where their career is concerned, that certainly should be publicized.

● *Can a one-line part on a television show help an unknown actor?*

No; I don't think the one line will do anything for him. But where I do think it's important is that he is working; he sees what is happening; he's learning his craft. He's watching the cameras and the lighting and the directors and other actors, and you can't pay enough for that experience. Also, he gets to work for a director, and that director may say to himself, "Gee, that actor is nice." The next time that director is doing a film, he may think of that actor for a bigger role. No, I don't think an actor who does not have the background should snub his nose at anything. Get on the set and work is my advice.

● *If an actor takes bit parts, does that work against him? Is he then thought of in those terms—a bit actor?*

It is all according to the way you say it. If you say it with, for example, "It was *only* a bit part," that's one thing, but if you say, "I know I only had a line, but it was my first shot," it's the actor's delivery that's important. If he's ashamed of the one line, he's going to give that impression.

● *We haven't discussed interviews. There are many good actors and actresses who just aren't good on interviews. What can they do to overcome this?*

There are many, many actors and actresses who are very shy and who really resent having to be interviewed. If this has become part of their personality, there is really no way that they are going to get around it. Hopefully one can see through it, and I think one normally can. Hopping around and meeting as many people as you can is what you should do in order to become known. If not, how do people get to know you? Study is of the utmost importance, but getting out and being in the company of people that can help is also very necessary.

● *Sometimes it seems as if good looks can be a detriment for a man today. How do you feel about it?*

Handsome could possibly have been out for a couple of years, but boy, I never get tired of seeing a good-looking man, and I don't think anybody else does, although it shouldn't always be the good-looking man, nor should it always be the unattractive man. I think it should be the right actor for the right part.

● *On the same subject, do you feel it's easier for a pretty girl via the casting couch?*

No, not the casting couch. There have been those actresses we've known that have tried the casting couch route and it hasn't worked, but I do believe a pretty girl has a far better opportunity because there are more parts written for a pretty girl. There's always the pretty girl next door, or the sex bombshell, or the whatever. A pretty girl with a pretty figure has a far better chance. There are not too many parts written for the ones that are not attractive.

● *Summing it all up, what are the main ingredients a young actor should have today in order to get ahead?*

The main ingredients. . . This will actually be a recap, but the main ingredient is the appeal, whatever it is—the sex appeal or the lovely appeal that Ryan O'Neal has, which to me isn't a sex appeal but just a lovely, super, boy-next-door appeal. You want to be around him. Or the appeal that Clint Eastwood has, which is a sex appeal, but also you know there's a man there that could handle anything—a "cool appeal." The ingredients put together are sex, nice, and cool—the three super ingredients that make up a successful actor. I think it's the appeal that makes you want to be with them or want to know them better, want to spend your time with them and not be wasting your time. It fulfills something inside of us. I think the same applies to the actress, even though I've mainly said "actor."

● *What are some of the things the actor does that may give him a bad reputation?*

Punctuality. If an actor comes in late, that goes around

very quickly. If he's rude and hard to work with, that too can be a detriment. Now that doesn't mean that the actor should just sit or stand there and not say anything. Quite to the contrary. If he's confused about something, he should talk to the director, or if he feels very strongly about a conceptual point, he should certainly discuss it. Most directors are terribly creative and will listen to the actor within reason. If the actor has a good point, they will often go along with it and try it. There are very few directors that won't do that, but the actor should not take advantage of it. In other words, it's not every line that should be discussed. "Do you think this? Do you think that?" *That* the director doesn't have time for. But, above all, the actor should be professional when he's working.

# Michael Campus
## Director

"I'm constantly praying that someone will come in when I'm casting and electrify me."

Directing a scene from *The Education of Sonny Carson.*

Michael Campus was born and raised in New York City. He graduated from the University of Wisconsin with a B.S. degree in journalism and soon after was commissioned as a lieutenant in the U.S. Army, in charge of U.S. military trains going through the Soviet zone of Germany. Returning home, he became one of the five producer-writers for "P.M. East—P.M. West" starring Mike Wallace. A short time later he joined ABC-TV to work as a documentary filmmaker for John Secondari and in the course of the next three years made four trips around the world working on such award-winning shows as "The Saga of Western Man" and the "Bell and Howell Close-up" series. He next went to CBS-TV as director of special programs and for the next three years was responsible for over 150 specials, among them "Death of a Salesman," "Sol Hurok Presents," and "The Glass Menagerie." In 1972 he decided to try the motion picture field. Since then, he has directed the following:

*Z.P.G.*
*The Mack*
*The Education of Sonny Carson*

Michael Campus . . . soft-spoken fraternity boy from back East makes good! And made good he has. Like Milton Katselas, Michael is of the new, young breed of directors. He is in his early thirties, is bespectacled, and has bushy hair. We listened over coffee to his ideas of what motion pictures *should* be all about—for Michael, a melding of all the elements, a marriage between everyone: the director, composer, cameraman, actors, grips, "go-fers," and so on. "Everyone should play a part," he says, "not just the actors."

*Michael Campus*

● *As a film director, Michael, what do you basically look for when you're casting?*

I think that truth is what casting is all about—truth is probably what movies are all about and so in casting I look for that quality we loosely call magic, something extraordinary that compels me, that attracts me—something in that human being sitting across from me that makes me want to jump up and say, "That's it!". If I find that quality and if I'm attracted and compelled by that person, then I think the audience will want to be compelled by them.

● *Is this thing you're looking for a physical quality?*

It's a non-intellectual thing and it took me a long time to understand that. In film fifty percent of what we get from a movie is chemical. We can't even explain it to each other. So, to me, if my gut tells me that something about *that* person is mesmerizing, that's what gets me even if I have to change a part—if I have to rewrite a scene or even rebuild a character, I will do that if I find somebody extraordinary.

● *That's very different from how most directors in Hollywood go about casting. Did you work that way in* The Mack?

Yes, completely and it's something that I'm now sworn to live by and die by and I'm constantly praying that someone will come in when I'm casting and electrify me. As outrageous as it sounds, I think that most interviews are over before the person speaks. For me, every bit of chemistry that's involved happens before they sit down or as they're sitting down or certainly after the first sentence and I know that's totally the opposite of what it is for ninety percent of what other directors feel and do, but to me, in terms of what I hope

167

to accomplish in the next few years, that's the core of it and I think that's why people watch films—why they're affected by films. If you grab them by the throat and they're moved—if they hate you or love you or whatever it is—fifty percent of that comes from casting and if they don't have the training I can teach them whatever they need to know.

● *You would cast a part to type then rather than an actor taking on the qualities of the part?*

Absolutely. I think that most casting that I've seen suggests to me that the directors work from outside in, instead of from inside out. They try to force the part onto a series of actors rather than working the other way and saying, "I have a project. I have a canvas. I have the colors that I need . . . now I have to shape those colors into a series of forms that will work for me." If ten people walk into my office and three of them are extraordinary but they don't fit the three parts I need, I will, as I said, rebuild those parts and it doesn't matter if those three people are complete unknowns.

● *Would you rather work with a non-professional actor or with a very experienced professional?*

I like to work with both but don't want to work with anybody, star or non-star who's been etched in concrete, who has become so rigid they're unable to break free. If they are rigid and they approach a role by saying, "Where do I stand?", if their first line to me is "Where's my mark, where do I go from here?" then it's dead and if that's the impression I get in an interview, then that person is automatically out for me and I don't care how big they are. It does not matter because I know I'm not going to get anything and conversely, I'm not going to give them anything.

● *Do you think it's better in certain roles, to use an unknown?*

Absolutely. The more open the channel is, the deeper the instrument, the actor's instrument. Obviously, there are actors that are so-called "stars" who are desperately waiting for the right part—waiting for the right moment and have never gotten it. It seems to me as if we've re-entered the star system era and this is going to be one of the things that directors are going to have to live with. If the star feels he is larger than the director and more meaningful at the box office, it suggests a lot of serious creative limitations.

● *In* Sonny Carson, *a lot of your actors weren't actors but members of the black gang and yet on film, it is impossible to tell who was an actor and who wasn't. How did you work with them to achieve that result?*

If *Sonny Carson* is a success, I would say it's because I was able to rehearse. The two weeks I rehearsed formulated the film. The film jelled during the rehearsal period because these kids had never acted before, and the key was the time spent in working with them until I had molded them and until I was able to infuse them with what I wanted and get back from them what they were capable of giving to me.

● *Then your way is really counter to the normal way of working as a director?*

Yes. I'm not interested in traditional means of casting in Hollywood, and I think if I'm going to be somewhat different as a director and create a different situation for myself, it will be because I've established a different method. In casting *Sonny Carson*, I opened up the doors to everyone in the black community of Bedford Stuyvesant. I saw fifteen hundred people in the course of six weeks. And I don't mean that I was lining up a hundred people at a time against a wall and saying, "I'll take you and you and you." I made index cards on every person, and I would read the people that I thought might have something. Also, I carry a notebook with me wherever I go, and in that notebook I document everything that I felt, that I saw, and out of this notebook came the reevaluation of the script.

● *What was your next step in casting after you saw all those people?*

What I did after I saw those fifteen hundred people was to stage a series of over a hundred improvisational exercises in which groups of the people I liked would put on little skits, and it was incredible. After ten or fifteen of these skits, certain themes would appear and reappear—a father returning home from prison and finding the mother with another man, the drug experience, the illegitimate child, prison, dope, reform school—and the kids themselves were acting out their lives, not their fantasies, and this helped me form what ended up on the screen.

● *Do you feel the young black actor is looser than the white actor?*

No. I think the reason I ended up making two black pictures is the newness of all of this. Films about the black experience are really only about five years old. The black film is a child in the motion picture world, and there is such vitality and such energy. There is such excitement, because it's the first time they are being allowed to escape Stepin Fetchit and really get into the life experience of their people. It is without a doubt akin to what the Jews felt at the turn of the century, which, by the way, was never adequately expressed. The black experience is a boiling pot that we've kept the lid on for all these years, and now suddenly the lid is off and people are going to say things about what happened. This is the great opportunity, and directors, writers, and actors are going to emerge, and that's extraordinary!

● *What do you think then is the role of the actor today? Is it to communicate the ideas of the writer and the director to the public?*

No, and I think that is one of the problems. A lot of directors talk about actors as being clay, and I think that is nonsense. I don't think any actor should be a tool of the director but a partner, and there should be a fusion of interests. It's an incredible sharing of ideas, and out of this comes the creative extension of yourself or the actor.

● *Let's go back to the actor in Hollywood and the various problems that beset him. If you were talking to young actors, what would you tell them?*

I think the biggest problem, and it's a tragedy in Hollywood—and here I have a damaging thing to say about directors—is that actors are starved for good parts, for understanding, and for knowledge. Most directors do not take the time, do not expend the energy, to deal with actors as people and give them the opportunity to really build something that's valuable. And this is the great tragedy of this town—that the opportunities are so scarce and television is such a numbing factor. I hear again and again from actors, "If someone would only direct me, if someone would only give me guidance, help me." So I think the answer to that is for the actor to seek out the people in life who are going to help him understand what the business is about. If I were an actor, I'd watch every director's work. I would select the director that I wanted to work with, and the younger he was, the better. I would park on his doorstep and I would do the same thing with a writer. I would get hold of the youngest, meanest writer I could find who has talent and I'd say, "Let's work together." I noticed in an article in *Time* magazine that Jack Nicholson roomed with Robert Towne, the writer of *Chinatown*, obviously a very fine writer, and out of that came an association. So instead of the actor just sitting back and saying, "Oh, my God, television is destroying me and I'm sitting in my crummy apartment not doing anything," I would actively try to gather people around me that will allow me to express my art. And to do that, besides going to class, you have to be able to find a writer, a director, and other people at that early stage that can help you.

● *Do you feel that experiencing life is as important as study or more so?*

That is part of the tragedy of the American actor. He's weaned on television, and in many cases he is unwilling to go out and experience and to gather experiences. I think one of the most important things in my life as a director was the year I lived in India. I spent the first three years of my profession directing and writing documentaries. I traveled around the world five times, and that taught me more about what I wanted to do and what I wanted to be than anything else that's happened to me in my life. That comes from living and experiencing, and without being trite about it, I don't think anything valid creatively is done without pain. I hope that's not shocking, but I think pain allows us to grow. I don't think anything is really achieved by not really getting involved.

● *Do you find other young directors feel this way today?*

No. That's what I find disappointing. There's all this

talk about the new Hollywood—all these articles about the new wave of people—and I find them emulating Hollywood as it's always been. I really don't see that courageous band of writers, producers, directors, and actors who are saying, "We're going to change everything and begin again with this incredible medium that we have." I see the form, the film form, returning back to what it was in the thirties, back to the basic forms as if to say, "Hooray for Hollywood! Let's get back to when movies were movies!" I guess there's some validity in that, but where are the people who are courageous enough and interested enough to say, "Let's break out and explore the new possibilities of our media"? I do not see the D. W. Griffiths and the Eisensteins of 1974.

● *Is there any filmmaker you respect besides yourself?*
   Oh, yes; there are a lot of people I respect, but the man I respect very much is Orson Welles. The interesting thing about him is that despite his recent failures, he is still trying things that are totally different and innovative. For example, his new film is involved with stills, newsreel footage, black-and-white, color, sixteen-millimeter and thirty-five-millimeter film. He dares to try, and I applaud him. I think he's marvelous.

● *What kind of static do you get when you are being financed by a studio if you want to use unknowns in the leads?*
   I think one of the shocking things about *The Education of Sonny Carson,* and I am still bewildered by it, was that I was left really alone. Frank Yablans, the former president of Paramount, has been my biggest fan, my mentor, and my friend. He let me go ahead and make the film I wanted to make. When I walked into Paramount, I had my jaw set thinking, "All right, you

guys, I'm going to fight you tooth and nail," and instead, I found a tremendous receptivity to do what I wanted to do.

● *With the success of* Sonny Carson, *do you find yourself as a director typecast to some extent?*

Yes, and it is dangerous. *The Mack* has been running for eighteen months, so I've done it twice successfully. There is a danger, and the only way for me to solve it is by simply saying I will not make another black film. Now if I make another film about the black experience, it will be because I wish to, not because I'm forced to.

● *Do you think we'll go back to the star system and then to the kinds of films required by that system?*

Apparently, because we seem to be in a depression-inflation cycle, and it correlates to the depression of the late twenties and early thirties. We seem to be returning to a kind of escapist pattern. I just wish people would stop making *Chinatown* and start making film that affects the times we live in. There were the people that said I couldn't make *Sonny Carson* because it's downbeat—it's depressing, and it shows a tragic side of life. They tell you to make a musical, make a western, make a comedy, and I think that's total nonsense. I think the only criterion for a filmmaker is to make what he believes in and wants to say and hope that he will get the money to make it. Film should be an experience, an extraordinary experience. Instead, the last five films I've seen have been dead. I don't think the audience felt anything at all. Jack Warner judged films by the number of times people got up and went to the bathroom or to buy candy. We had some showings of *Sonny Carson* and every night at least fifteen people walked out in one scene because they couldn't bear it, and that's terrific. It means that whether they love it or hate it, there's a reaction. If they're appalled by what I've done, then that means that I've done my job. I don't care if people love me or hate me as long as they're moved.

● *What you're saying then is that film must go forward with the times, and that's not what you've seen happening?*

I don't see anybody extending the medium—extending the form. When the *nouvelle vague* happened a few years back, our whole vision of film changed. It was like an explosion. There were subliminal cuts, different forms, but now there seems to be a kind of lethargy in which nobody seems to know what to try.

● *The only new form seems to be the porno film, doesn't it?*

Yes.

● *Do you feel it's necessary for the director to work with the writer?*

It's impossible to make a great film unless that's done, and unfortunately in many cases it isn't. Usually the writer finishes his work, kisses it goodbye, and then the director comes in, puts his stamp on the picture, and walks off with it. Another item that's unbelievable is that music is the last thing that happens in a film. It's idiocy of the highest order. The composer should be brought along the first day and live the experience with the director and writer, and he should be composing out of the experience, out of the heat rising from the pavements as in the case of *Sonny Carson*. He should emerge from the experience, and he in turn can stimulate the director.

● *What is your dream in film?*

My dream would be to have my own film company in which everybody would be totally involved in the creation, because making a film is like giving birth to a child. You get pregnant and wildly excited and you anguish and agonize over those nine months, and at the end you give birth. And yes, one of the fingers is slightly deformed, and one of the features is bent, but something about that child makes you cry and laugh and soar, and that's the beauty of it. There is a way to do that, and it can be done.

● *Have you ever worked on a film where there was a personality clash between two actors?*

Yes; it happened to me on my first film. Now I have reached the point where I will not work with anyone unless everyone has met beforehand and I know everyone gets along and is on the same brain wave. Too often films are stuck together with porous glue—the star and director are tacked on from one place, the art director from somewhere else. These people have never met, don't know each other, and maybe don't feel anything for each other, and yet they are supposed to work together as some incredible team. That's nonsense. Again, the concept of a film company where everybody digs each other comes up, but what defeats that is the economics.

Oftentimes I've been asked what I want. Money is not what I'm after. I'm after sufficient strength so I can dictate the terms that I work under, and that means having my own group of people. I love the idea of the *auteur,* the filmmaker, except that it doesn't make much sense. Great filmmaking comes from teams of people that all contribute to each other. A great film comes out of a great director but also a great script writer, a great costume designer, great actors, great composers, great production managers. I'll even go further than that and say a great gaffer, a great grip. It's true, the director has to have the vision, but without the other people, without that cohesion, you may as well forget it. If I'm going to achieve something within this industry, I cannot achieve it by myself. Part of it will be because I am capable of selecting those who have as much to offer as I do.

# Meyer Mishkin
## Talent Agent

"As soon as there is a demand for your services,
you can write your own ticket."

Meyer Mishkin was born in New York City on February 12, 1912. He completed his education at CCNY. Since then, he has been a talent scout and casting director for Twentieth Century-Fox and a partner in the Huntington Hartford Agency. In 1956, with Jeff Chandler, he formed Earlmar Productions for the purpose of producing the film *Drango*. He has represented and helped develop the careers of Jeff Chandler, Charles Bronson, Peter Graves, James Coburn, and Lee Marvin. He is still representing many more television and motion picture personalities.

Meyer Mishkin sat in his office on Sunset Boulevard. He is a short, plump man who should, himself, be playing the role of Happy in a performance of *Snow White and the Seven Dwarfs*. His whole life has been and still is show business, and as he reflects on the "good old days," his face lights up. Despite the number of years he has been in the business, Meyer Mishkin has lost none of his enthusiasm for his work nor his love for the actor. Unlike the giant agencies such as IFA, CMA, or the Morris Agency, Meyer Mishkin is the epitome of the smaller agent whose life is one of the utmost dedication to his clients. Although one suspects he has been hurt by the kind of disloyalties all agents are subject to, he is not the least bit bitter. Over the years he has represented many of the top stars. One, Lee Marvin, has remained a loyal and true client for over twenty years, while others have come and gone.

● *Can you tell us briefly how you started in the motion picture business and how you finally ended up being one of the top agents?*

I first started at a firm called the Fox Case Corporation that was in the business of making newsreels and was based in New York. My first job was running errands for twelve dollars a week while attending school at night. This was during the depression. It was during a period when Fox was in the process of making screen tests of stage personalities and had the only studios in town at that time. The first screen test I ever saw was of Jimmy Cagney and Joan Blondell doing a scene from a play they were then doing on Broadway called *Penny Arcade,* and Jimmy actually did the same dance that he did in *Yankee Doodle Dandy.* Twentieth Century-Fox turned them down!

During this same period MGM rented the same studio space and proceeded to test such people as Robert Montgomery, Henry Fonda, Jimmy Stewart. Some of them were taken; others were not. Bob Hope made his test there, and a little later, Paul Muni. I was the guy who would take them to the dressing room and carry the bag upstairs, et cetera, so my background actually started right there. After a while I started to help a fellow who was a talent scout there and I commenced to cover the various little theater groups around New York. This was around 1931-32, and in those days the term Broadway was not used. It was little theater; it was dramatic school; it was the Academy of Dramatic Arts; the American Academy, the New York School of the Theatre, the Neighborhood Playhouse, and a number of others, and all the would-be thespians went to those schools. After the actor studied at one of these schools he would serve an apprenticeship in stock, and I would cover all the summer stock theaters, too. Actually, I didn't start doing that till 1936, when they transferred me into the talent department. I would travel up and down the coast seeing shows from Maine down to Miami and across country as far as Chicago's Goodman Theatre. I sometimes watched players for as much as two years in various things before I even recommended them for screen tests. It was a little different from today, as now it seems as soon as an actor graduates from a university drama department he wants to be a star. In those days it was actually like going through a baseball buildup where you worked in the sandlots and then got to the Class D baseball, then into C and finally B and, only then, into the National League before you went to the pro leagues. In those days you really had to work at it.

● *Can an actor coming directly out of a drama school become a star if he gets the right break?*

Only in freak instances, because I do not believe anyone becomes a star out of one film. The industry may try to push them into that area with publicity, but the public just doesn't remember their names after one film.

● *Isn't that part of the problem today—that the young actor doesn't get the proper guidance, that many agents push them?*

Oh, sure; I find there are many agents who have had no background whatsoever in the theater, in motion pictures, or show business. They come from some other field, and all they do is negotiate deals. They don't guide, don't direct their people, and my attitude about agenting is "I want to help make motion pictures," and I don't want to negotiate against it. I want to help the director and the producer make the film. In other words, if I can contribute through my actor, then I'm part of the film. And I think this is why I talk to directors and producers constantly; this is why I've got scripts piled up all over the place—because they feel that I'm trying to contribute instead of just trying to make a deal.

● *You have represented Lee Marvin from the very beginning of his career.*

Lee Marvin was introduced to me by Henry Hathaway. I had been with Hathaway as his casting director on such films as *House on 92nd Street, 13 Rue Madeleine, Call Northside 7777,* and *Kiss of Death.* (I'd also worked with Elia Kazan on *Boomerang, Gentlemen's Agreement,* et cetera, and I'm just mentioning this because it was the background for learning how to communicate with actors, how to deal with them, and how, as I say, to contribute.)

Hathaway had brought Lee from New York for a bit part in the film *U.S.S. Tea Kettle,* which Gary Cooper was starring in, and I, having just become an agent, went over to the set. Actually, Henry had tried to stop me from becoming an agent and wanted me to work out here for Fox. Henry introduced me to Lee on the set, saying, "This guy's good and I want you to sign him." I replied, "Can I watch him do something?" Lee was then about twenty-five. Henry got angry that I wouldn't take his word for it. I said, "Henry, when I was casting pictures for you, you always asked me if I'd seen the actor work." He turned to Lee and said, "Look, I'm trying to get you an agent. You know these two lines. I want you to do them." Lee said, "OK." Even then he was relaxed, real cool, and nothing fazed him.

So I watched him do a scene and I said, "Yes, I'll sign him." Lee then turned to me and said, "Any agent that can get me two lines that quickly in a part that had no lines—I'm with you!"

And that's how I started with Lee, and that was Christmas, 1949. As soon as he had finished his part in that film he said he was going back to New York, and as I didn't have time to introduce him around to casting directors, et cetera, I came up with a good idea. I suggested he help me deliver my Christmas presents to the various staff at all the studios—I remember we went to six studios in one day—and then he left for New York. But every time I brought his name up at the studios, they all remembered him. "Oh," they said, "the guy who brought in the presents!" When he called me to tell me he was coming back to Hollywood, I immediately called the studios and they still remembered him. It's not easy to remember anyone for any period of time, but Lee just had that quality. There was no question about it. He was cool, completely relaxed in appearance—not inwardly, but outwardly. I don't believe there's another actor in the business who went from scale wages to a million dollars a film.

● *But isn't your relationship with Lee one of the rare ones between actor and agent? It's like one of the few good marriages.*

Very definitely. Recently someone said to me, "Gee, it must be tough handling Marvin." I replied, "The easiest representation I have is Lee Marvin. He's never once raised his voice to me, and we've been together now for over twenty years."

● *At this time and place in motion pictures and television would you take on the representation of an unknown actor?*

Only—and I mean only—if that unknown intrigues

me. Until recently I've always worked with a certain number of unknowns. Over the years there were many. Jeff Chandler was a radio actor. I had known him as Ira Grossell at a playhouse in Long Island when he was doing stock. In those days Jeff was tall and gaunt and, although only in his early twenties, starting to get a little gray. During that period at Twentieth the only people who were tested were those that looked like Tyrone Power, and Jeff didn't fit that category. I brought in Gregory Peck from the Neighborhood Playhouse, and they made a silent screen test. Can you imagine making a silent screen test of Gregory Peck and him with that vocal quality!

● *Did they sign him?*

No. Now let's talk about the first screen test that Marlon Brando ever made. I brought him in from the New School of Social Research. My boss at the time said, "What will we do with him? He can't talk; he's crazy; and he has a funny nose." I finally prevailed upon them to do an interview test of him and they junked it. I watched Brando after that. I went to New Haven and saw him do *I Remember Mama*. The reviewers destroyed it because there were so many technical difficulties, but then it came to New York and was a big hit. I continued watching him, saw him do *Truck Line Cafe*, which, to me, was the best performance I ever saw him do, and on and on. We've kept giggling together at what has happened with his career, but in the beginning Fox wouldn't have him. None of the companies would have him in that period.

● *Are the studios still that narrow-minded about actors who are different?*

There's a whole different area today. There are no companies that sign people and put them under term contracts. The only company that still works in that direction is Universal, and their attitude about doing it is: Who fits into the possibility of going into a television series?

● *So they really don't look for anybody who is truly different and unique?*

No.

● *Do you feel that the star—a Paul Newman, a Robert Redford, or a Lee Marvin—is coming to an end?*

No. But it's never going to be the same ratio as it was years ago when people would go to see a Cary Grant, a Gary Cooper, or a Bogart picture. There were only a certain number of films during that period that one would see, and you didn't have the competition that you have today. Today we have audiences that watch basketball, hockey, and other sports instead of going to the theater. If you check into basketball in colleges, you'll find that seven or eight years ago you couldn't give away a game on television, and today basketball games proliferate on weekends during the basketball season.

● *Nobody really makes it overnight, so to speak, do they? It takes a steady building of a career.*

You mean like Jimmy Caan or Burt Reynolds or Gene Hackman. Burt Reynolds had been in four series before he was successful, and the others I just mentioned, as you know, have had years and years of both hard work and rejection.

● *Originally Lee Marvin played heavies, didn't he? What do you think was the turning point in his career?*

When I suggested Lee doing comedy, they'd say, "Oh, no; he's too much the heavy. He's a mug." I know this interview is about the industry and not about me, but let

me just tell you my theory. Over the years I've
represented Jeff Chandler, Charles Bronson (whose
name I changed from Brojinski because the only thing
they ever called him for was to play Polish coal miners or
something similar), Lee Marvin, Chuck Connors, and
Jimmy Coburn. All were under the category of leading
men in the Player's Directory, and whenever a casting
director told me they were character people, which was
often, I would say that there were no character people if
the personality of the individual doubled your audience.

● *Don't you feel that personality is sex appeal, especially in
all those men that you've mentioned?*

Sure it is, but you don't find that out talking to some of
the casting directors.

● *Say you found some new young actor that you were trying
to sell today in a certain way. Does the casting director still
have a set idea about categories?*

You will always have walls, not only with casting
directors but with directors and producers and especially a writer who is also directing. When he writes, he
already has certain people set in his mind for certain
roles, and if you bring in somebody else, it will bother
him. Sometimes they feel you're out of your mind for
suggesting somebody. It's frustrating because you
know how adept actors are, that they can play lots of
parts because they are strong and capable.

● *Do you suggest to your clients that they do plays, work on
stage?*

Sure, but I don't particularly believe in using the phrase
"I've learned my craft," because if anyone says to me
that he learned his craft, I am inclined to believe that
he's almost stopped learning. I think he should just go
do it and not talk about it. Actors will sometimes call

me when they've finished a job to tell me, "They like me—just one take," and I'll say, "But was it good?" They must realize that it's better to have twenty takes and get a good one! A thing happens to actors, and nine out of ten of them have that problem. For instance, they do well on stage, but when they start working in film or in television, there's something back there in their head that says, "If it doesn't work out right, they'll do it again." So psychologically they have that to fall back on, whereas they would never think of it that way if they had to make an entrance on stage where they have to give their best performance and be thoroughly prepared. But when it comes to film, and especially if they have achieved some position in the industry, they tend not to do their best. It's the actor who approaches it just as if he were doing a play, never thinking that he'll walk through it because they'll do it again—I think he's the guy that eventually comes through.

● *Actors seem, as a whole, to have a bad reputation in the area of loyalties. What is your feeling on this?*

Basically loyal? I think they are more susceptible than people in any other business, more susceptible to flattery or, shall we say, false flattery. But you would be surprised, more often than not, it's the wife. She persuades the actor to come into the office to inform the agent that he's outgrown him, that although the agent's been wonderful, for the sake of his career, he must go with the larger agency. It's the wife most of the time who puts the idea into her husband's head, because she's the one who wants to read in the trade papers that they've been seen at some celebrity fund-raising dinner party sitting at the table with so-and-so. Do you know what I mean?

● *Have you ever dealt with an actor who left you to go with the large agency just as his career was beginning to take an upward turn, only to find himself lost and missing the personalized representation that only the good smaller agency can give?*

I certainly have, and I'd prefer not talking about it. An example, and I won't mention any names: A client had gotten to the point where he was getting big money, and the larger agencies were beginning to woo him. He finally succumbed, left me, and went with the largest. For two years he was with the biggest agency in this town and it just didn't work. Finally, when he did go back to work, he earned, I would say, one-fourth of the money per picture he was earning when he was with me.

● *After you find a good new actor who you decide to take on as a client, how long does it take for him to make some kind of living in his profession? In other words, is there a time limit one should set for oneself?*

Look, I won't promise anybody anything. If I'm a good house painter and I say, "I'll do a good job for you," that's one thing. But if I have to rely on other people to hire the actor, then I can't promise him anything.

● *Then how long before you give up a client?*

I hardly ever give up on a client until I feel he stops progressing or his attitude is wrong. For example, I first saw Richard Dreyfus when he was just fifteen at a little theater called The Player's Ring. He's now twenty-four, and here again is something in keeping with what I said earlier—that people do not remember an actor's name from one film. Richard Dreyfus was the only actor in the short life of the Los Angeles theater critics to be nominated for two plays in one season. He did a musical at the Theatre West Company, and he did *Time of Your Life* with Hank Fonda and Struther Martin, and *he* was the one nominated in the play. He now has three unreleased pictures which will be coming out shortly, and he played in the film *Catch 22* for Paramount. Although they paid him a lot of money for that film, over all these years there has been very little income. He has struggled with it, and I have too. He will tell you himself how often he's said, "Meyer is the only person I know that came down to Beverly Hills High School to see me," and my answer is, "When I believe in someone, I've got to do something about it."

● *Isn't it a little easier if the actor is a little older? Can he sometimes be too young?*

It all depends. Some people are more adaptable to screen, whether it's television or motion pictures, when they get older. For instance, Lee today, with the gray hair, has much more appeal. As a matter of fact, today you won't believe Lee as a heavy like in those days.

● *And James Coburn?*

Well, Coburn's problem was that he became almost a hippie, but he was already too old to be a hippie. You can't go around saying "Man," wearing beads, and so forth and have the younger people look at you and say, "Get him."

● *Did Charles Bronson's phenomenal success over the last few years surprise you?*

No. Charlie's an animal. The muscles are on the face, and there's this whole physical thing going. There's not a looseness about Charlie; there's a tautness. For instance, Lee Marvin can make a point with just a look or a movement of an eye. With Charlie, the cheeks tighten up. Strangely enough, the public really can't tell a good actor from an ordinary one, but they know what pleases them.

● *Summing up, what are the young actor's chances of making it as a working actor today compared to five years ago?*

I think his chance of working in the industry is better today than it used to be, but his chances of becoming successful in it—really successful—are more difficult. Although there are many more television shows being made, there is a proliferation of new directors, and a new director from his perspective and his ego says, "I can take new people and I can make them act." Therefore it gives the newcomer more of a chance to be used, and this does open the door. But the quality of work isn't very high, let me tell you. I saw a pilot for a new television show the other day. It's sold, and I heard them talking about this young girl in it. They were saying how darling she was, and all I could think was, "Yes, she's darling all right, but she's also a klutz. She can't even walk properly." And I know they were constantly shooting away from her because they just couldn't keep the camera on her. After putting her into the lead in that pilot, they are now sending her to dramatic school!

But the most important thing for the young actor is attitude. He *must* have the feeling that somewhere along the line he is going to achieve stardom, and he *must* approach it that way. I do believe that for those people that work at it and learn—learn in relationship to their own capacity, own personality (and it's not like learning addition and subtraction, it goes way beyond that), I believe if the young actor keeps doing this, somewhere along the line something will open up for him and he'll have the opportunity. But *he has to believe*. It's like my attitude in reference to salaries. Do the job and then the money will come. As soon as there is a demand for your services, you can write your own ticket.

# David Dortort
## Producer-Writer

"No part is too unimportant. All the actor needs is that one moment to make something work for him."

David Dortort was born in New York City on October 23, 1916, and began his long, successful career as a novelist and short story writer. He created and produced two of the most successful television shows ever—"Bonanza" and "High Chapparal." He has received both the National Heritage Award and the coveted Hall of Fame Award, and he has been nominated twice for a television Emmy. David Dortort taught a course in creative writing at the University of California, Los Angeles. He is a former president of the television branch of the Writers' Guild of America and former president of the Producers' Guild of America.

David Dortort is a tall, thin man in his early sixties who has made nothing but money from his creativity in the television industry. He is one of the most highly respected producer-writers in the business. Quiet, but exuding great authority, he came to our office to give us the "lowdown" on working in television.

● *What do you look for in an actor?*

I look for a kind of technical training. It's a plus, and, even beyond that, working in some of the theaters in town is very healthy. I see as much theater as is humanly possible. In fact, I have chosen some very important people from that sort of exposure. However, I feel acting classes and workshops really don't relate to the main currents that are updated in the industry at any particular time. They've very specialized—over-specialized—due, I think, to the people that teach. Unfortunately, many of the teachers in these work-shops are not quite attuned to the current trends in the industry.

● *As the producer of two of the most successful shows on television, have you given breaks to many young actors?*

Yes. I think possibly more than anyone in the business. I started Dan Blocker as an actor. I picked Henry Darrow out of a little theater where I saw him give a magnificent performance in a Ray Bradbury play. I hired Richard Thomas before he had many credits. I don't look for a long list of credits as an essential, though it's useful.

● *Have you ever seen a face that interested you and, without knowing anything about that person's ability, think you wanted to meet that actor?*

That's how I came to find Mark Slade. His agent brought me a picture. He looked very, very interesting. He came in that afternoon and I gave him a part in "High Chapparal." It doesn't happen too often.

● *Is it easier for a young actor to break into feature films than television?*

TV people, due to pressures such as tight schedules, et

cetera, like to go by what they call "the insurance factor." Sometimes they don't even have time to read an actor or do a thorough casting interview, and so they go on the basis of previous TV credits, whereas in a motion picture, there's more stress given to a reading and rehearsal time and the young actor has more of a chance.

● *Milt Hammerman was your casting director for many years. Did you rely on his judgment? Who has final say on casting—you, the producer, or the director?*

Well, it goes this way. Primary responsibility is on the casting director, as it should properly be. However, on any individual show, the director is also very closely consulted, and what generally happens is that the two of them come to some agreement—maybe after a series of disagreements—and bring their final list of recommendations to me. I accept all, part, or in some cases, none. This is due to the fact that my own knowledge in terms of performers is rather extensive.

● *Let's go back to the young actor who is just out of drama school and has no film or professional credits. How would he go about getting a job on a television show?*

The best way, simply because he's set up to handle it, is to try and contact the casting director. Occasionally, if someone I know has a very high opinion of an actor and he or she feels this performer should get my special attention and I have the time—and generally I will find the time in spite of a terribly busy schedule—I will give a personal reading. However, the actor should not wait for that sort of thing but find an opportunity to act and showcase himself wherever he can. I cannot stress how useful the little theater approach is. I go to all of them.

● *Do you think you're special in doing that?*
Rather, but I generally find many casting people there
and it's fun to compare notions. I think it has served me
well. I've found some tremendously interesting talent.
● *Have you ever given an unknown actor a good part on one
of your shows only to have it backfire?*
Unfortunately, it does happen. Sometimes I'm carried
away by my enthusiasm for either a stage performance
or a specially vivid reading and, of course, my sympathy
is always with the actor. I love them all, knowing how
difficult a path they've chosen. Occasionally, I find my
own judgment clouded by that fact.

Lack of experience and poise in front of a camera
can be a terribly frustrating experience. Sometimes an
actor is so wedded to a particular method of teaching
that he cannot free himself from it. Then comes the
conflict between that method of acting and the
director's concept of how the scene should go. If the
director is not sympathetic, and few of them are because
of the pressure of time, almost always the actor will be
hurt. I remember Jack Lord in his early days. He was so
locked into "the method" he literally drove everyone
crazy. He felt he needed that as a crutch to lean on, and I
had many, many long talks with him. On the other
hand, a man like Henry Darrow, with his superb
training in the theater, was able to adapt immediately.
He had such flexibility and as a result was very, very
interesting in front of the camera.

I think in the beginning two things are very
important. One is the willingness to listen, because the
inflexibility of coming from another medium can be
terribly confining and frustrating to everyone, and then

there is a willingness to work with other people, the receptivity to ideas.

● *Obviously, then, it's easier for an actor who has a pleasant, easygoing personality with the ability to mingle socially rather than the introverted person.*

I think it's helpful, though too much stress shouldn't be put on it, In the beginning it's important, but later on, when a person begins to develop skills and self-confidence, it doesn't matter as much. I remember bringing Joan Hackett out from New York. Everybody on the set thoroughly detested her because she was quiet and aloof. The director was completely baffled by her, but she turned in an exceptionally fine, wonderful performance. I made them all look at it and told them, "This is the woman you all said couldn't get along with anybody, but look at her performance on the screen." This has happened a number of times.

● *Do you think that most directors, producers, casting people, and so on have the ability to look at an actor and see him in any kind of part other than one that is suggested by his looks or that is like parts he has played in the past?*

We had a classic experience with that a few years ago. Stella Stevens, at that time the sex symbol of Hollywood, was not doing particularly well. I had a part in one of my films of a very simple girl, a deaf-mute who lived up in the mountains. When I suggested to Bob Altman, the director, that we use Stella, he thought I was crazy. Stella had heard about the part and had come to see me wearing a dress cut down to her navel. I told her how to dress, and she came back the next day wearing a simple dress and no makeup. I hardly recognized her. Altman didn't know who she was until I told him it was Stella. She read for us and was lovely. It started a whole new career for her. She became somebody just when she was on the road to becoming nobody.

● *But if Stella had walked in as an unknown actress, she wouldn't have been called back for a second interview.*

That's true. Unfortunately, there's just not enough time. I'd have to spend the better part of the day and night just casting.

● *In recent years, who really excites you as an actor?*

When I first used Richard Thomas, I built the show around him because I liked the quality he had. He'd done a very small part in *Winning* with Paul Newman and came off with a lot of charm. I brought him in. The part was a little mature and I wondered if he could rise to it, but he was wonderful. I suggested to NBC that we sign him, but they found him just another young actor! Well, now he's found his niche in "The Waltons." He's one of the most exciting young actors I've seen.

● *When an actor takes a running part in a TV series, isn't it then awfully difficult when he leaves that series to get parts different from what he's been playing?*

I'd like to answer that question by injecting something ahead of it. First of all, I think it's the most useful thing in the world that can happen to any actor—the chance to work on a series regularly. It's a workshop, a drama school, everything rolled into one. It's an apprenticeship under the best conditions, right in front of the camera, and for the young actor that's the important thing, even more important than the money and everything else, because if there's any talent, this will prove it, and he will grow and he will leave the series after three or five years infinitely superior to when he came in. Now, addressing myself to your question specifically, I think some actors have difficulty avoiding typecasting. It's not impossible, but what happens is that the industry starts to think of them in that mold. They've done it so well, why don't they do it again? And they fall into that trap.

● *Does publicity bring actors to the attention of people like yourself?*

I really don't think it's of much use even though it may bring you to someone's attention, because you finally have to have *"it."* So what happens after you've got someone's attention? If you have "it," you don't have to resort to that sort of expediency of going in for expensive photos, portfolios, taking ads in the trade papers. I've seen cases where young girls in particular will invest a fortune in that sort of stuff. I think they're being taken.

● *Do you use the Player's Directory when you're casting?*

Yes. I use it as I think everyone does. It's very useful. Now there, in terms of publicity, I think that it is very necessary for every actor and actress to have his picture and his agency recorded there, because we thumb through it all the time. In addition, actors should not be allowed to choose their own photos for the book, because they invariably select the most inappropriate one or something that is ancient vintage, not the straight shot which shows them as they are. The shock of seeing the difference when they come in for an interview! Immediately you think, "My God, I've been fooled!" I also find that kind of interview can be disastrous. Just a simple, straight, honest shot revealing what it should reveal, a close-up of the face, because the face tells everything. This is really an industry of

close-ups. You have to come in close finally. You have
to see if the expression is there, in the eyes.

● *Have you ever put someone in a very minor role then
given him larger roles because he was good?*

That was the story of Dan Blocker. He started with a
one-line part in "The Restless Gun," and I brought
him back again and again and again because there was
no end to his talent and his development. And this man
had never acted before. I wrote the part of Hoss with
him in mind when I was putting "Bonanza" together,
so you can see, no part is too small. No part is too
unimportant. All the actor needs is that one moment to
make something work for him. It doesn't happen all the
time, but sometimes it does.

● *Are the opportunities for a young actor today better than
they were five years ago?*

It isn't quite as good for these reasons: there are fewer
shows being made and fewer episodes being filmed.
Reruns of old movies have affected television to the
point where the opportunities are rare. I know some
excellent actors, character actors with good reputa-
tions. They'll get one or two jobs a year. It's
heartbreaking. Also, due to television, there's been an
increase in the actor's pool. It has attracted many more
actors to Hollywood than ever before. There's a great
deal of talent around, but that doesn't mean there isn't
an opportunity for a very exciting young actor or a
hard-working, determined young actress. I think it will
always prove to be so.

● *Does the television network have any say regarding
casting?*

Not with me they don't! I was completely autonomous

in my operation, but the truth of the matter is that they do have quite a bit of say, particularly in choosing leads on a series. I don't think they get that involved in guest star situations, but I may be wrong because on reflection, I do recall friends of mine in the industry having to send lists of recommendations to network people. Of course, they would never dare to interfere with my operation.

# Ethel Winant

## Casting Director

"God knows, we're not here *not* to give actors jobs."

208

Ethel Winant was born in Worcester, Massachusetts, but grew up in Marysville, California. She is a graduate of the University of California at Berkeley and holds a master of arts degree from Whittier College in California. She started working in the entertainment business in New York, where she eventually became head of casting for Talent Associates. With CBS since 1956, she was associate producer on their "Playhouse 90" series. She served as casting director on the original "Perry Mason" series, was associate producer of "General Electric Theatre," producer of "The Great Adventure" series, and assistant director of program development. In 1964 she was appointed director of casting in Hollywood, and in 1973 she was appointed to the newly created post of Vice President, Talent and Casting, Hollywood.

Ethel Winant is dedicated to her work as head of casting at Columbia Broadcasting Studios. A slight, middle-aged woman who is finely attuned to the actor, she knows all the tricks, all the signs, and quickly scrutinizes to see if that "spark" exists. She gives a hard interview, doesn't seem to unbend much, and tries, in this way, to bring the actor out. On first meeting with her, you get an impression that she is rather reserved, a feeling that she is "not to be fooled with." But there's a soft spot to Ethel, and once you've hit it she'll really go to bat for you. But you've got to be a true actor. As she herself says, "That's vital."

● *What are the opportunities for the actor today compared with five years ago?*

There's probably less opportunity today because of the reduction of television production, and most young actors get their first opportunity in television. There's less work, and there are so many actors in the industry it's just horrible. Also, budgets are a problem. They cast faster. There isn't so much time on preproduction; therefore, people tend to use actors they've used before. The biggest opportunity for the actor today is in the new films made by the young filmmakers and in underground movies where they don't want familiar faces. But the great amount of work that was offered to young actors, which overwhelmed all of us, belongs to the period a few years back when this enormous machine, TV, was grinding out product all the time and you constantly needed new people. The actors came into the business and worked instantly, many times when they weren't even prepared, because we were so desperate. The machine ate them up so fast. It's less now.

● *Do you have specific hours when you see young actors?*

Yes. We see twenty-five to thirty new actors a week. It's nowhere near enough.

● *If you do see a young actor with stage credits but no film, is there any possibility of your using him or her?*

Yes. First of all, I don't like to look at film because film is too deceptive. It's like looking at somebody's credits on the screen and saying, "It's a marvelous script," but you find out it's been rewritten seven times by the story editor. You really don't know. It also depends on the director, and somebody can come off very badly on film because it's been badly directed—particularly young actors who have no way of protecting themselves or who are absolutely marvelous if they have one of those super directors who can even work with people off the street. All you're seeing is a result, the work of several people, and all film ever tells me is how they look on camera. It isn't going to tell me anything about them as actors.

● *Do you read them?*

We read them, yes. One of the problems with young people is they come into the business with a wonderful naive attitude: "I'm an actor, and when I get on that stage or in front of that camera, I'm going to be wonderful." What they don't know is that the most important part is what is going to happen in an office like this or in a reading, and for that there should be a course called "The Interview." There should be a course in how to read, because that's what it's all about. I tell young actors that ninety percent of the time is spent in offices, and maybe, if they're lucky, ten percent will be spent doing what they really think they should be doing, and that's acting! This is acting—what happens when you come into this office, how you interview. The casting director can't remember everybody in the world. Try and sit down after a cocktail party and remember twenty people. It's no different for us. The actor that makes some sort of impact on an interview is the one you're going to remember. I can be wrong, too. It can mean that they are just great in a room, a smash hit at a party, but at least I'm going to remember them. When we're doing a specific show, we'll see ten, twenty, thirty people a day. That's a lot of people, and over a period of a week it really adds up. If the actor doesn't make a contribution to the interview, if he comes in and expects you to do the work, you end up saying, "What have you done?" because we're too tired and we're not imaginative enough to keep creating new conversational gambits with everyone that comes in. The actor that comes in and is full of himself or something, even if it's just that he got a car or has just read the newspaper, that's a conversation opener, and through that you can talk. If you don't have anything to say, make it up!

I keep saying to young actors, "You're an actor. Create a personality that comes to the interview. You've got to, because I can't do it over and over and over again." So in the end if the actor walks into my office and sits there in that chair and answers in monosyllables and is obviously annoyed because I'm asking dumb questions, then nothing's going to happen. Finally I have stopped feeling guilty about that. It's really his job to make it interesting for me. I don't want to offend them. I don't want to hurt people's feelings, and I don't want them leaving the room saying, "God, it was really terrible," but there's just so much you can do. I'm bored trying to draw out someone that comes in hostile.

One of the first things they must learn is that we're as desperate as they are. We pray every time that door opens that that person is going to be the new star of a new TV series. God knows, we're not here *not* to give actors jobs. We only look good by making new discoveries, finding new people. That's why we work. That is the function of a casting department. Otherwise, a director can just take the Academy Player's Directory and look for someone who looks like the part. They don't need us. So we do want them to be marvelous, but sometimes after you've had a whole week of interviews and they really are dreadful, you lose heart. Now and then I'll see a piece of work from an actor and I'll say, "I don't remember him." And sure enough, he was in my office, sitting over there staring at the wall, and he gave me nothing.

I think that's one of the actor's most important tools—interviews—because the first thing they're going to do is go on a general interview, and if they learn to make themselves interesting, as long as they have the energy, really that's what it's all about, a kind of theatrical energy, a kind of theatrical life. That's the difference between a guy who's never going to make it and a guy who's going to be a star.

● *Do you feel a "look" is important?*

No. We've really got away from that. The way it used to be, the perfect actor was somewhere between Rock Hudson and John Gavin, and all the ladies were supposed to look like Kim Novak. I think that's over, mainly due to the young filmmakers, who've stopped going for the kind of synthetic look. You are no longer locked into what we call "conventional beauty." All leading men in the old days of TV looked like Chad Everett. Now it's Peter Falk or Bill Conrad. It's personalities. Of course, I don't think it hurts, when one of those girls comes in and she has wonderful bones, great eyes, and you say, "Hey, that's something! She'd look good on the screen."

● *Is there a difference in TV actors as opposed to feature films?*

Not so much now. I think that movies have changed so much that they're interchangeable—TV and features.

● *Are most of the actors that come in for interviews usually sent by agents, or do they come by themselves?*

If you don't see all the people sent by agents, the agents hate you. We do try to see people who don't have agents, too. We hold auditions—not as often as we should, but we try to have them. Most of the time it's terribly disappointing.

● *Why?*

It's the old story. Anybody can say he's an actor. You need no credentials. You can't say you're a doctor or a lawyer unless you have a diploma, but anybody can say he's an actor.

● *If you were an actor starting out today, what steps would you take in order to make the most of an acting career?*

Well, starting from the very beginning, I would try and pick a good school with a good drama department—Northwestern, Carnegie Tech, maybe The Academy, maybe the Playhouse. They get you on the stage. They get you working. You're learning your own craft, being taught, and also you're performing. I would do stock, any stock. You learn by doing. It's a profession that must be practiced. Unfortunately, in Hollywood a girl can walk in, and because she has a certain quality and looks marvelously photogenic, the director can say, "Who cares if she can act?" and she could become a star overnight. Then, again, I'm not talking about that wonderful, weird thing, the person who is so loaded with talent that it comes out of every pore. Those come along very few times—the natural, perfect actor. But those are the exceptions.

The workmanlike actors should go to school, work at an interchange of ideas with other actors. The discipline of rehearsals is terribly important. Then try regional theater. You need that kind of experience, being on a stage, playing with audiences. Nothing will take the place of that, because the audience tells you what you're doing, right or wrong. That's the greatest barometer in the world. Either they're listening or they're not listening; either they're laughing or they're not laughing. By the time you come to enter the so-called profession, you have some skills and some background. Your tools are in shape, and you can now use them. You can respond to the requirements of the director. If you're prepared, I think you can begin. It's a pleasure to meet New York actors. They come into your office. They tell you what they've been doing, and nobody says, "I won't read." They're professional actors, and they believe if you want a job, you read for it. It's part of the trade to do it. I love their attitude. I love to go back to New York. It's so easy. It's marvelous! You meet all those wonderful "up" people. They may go out feeling terrible, but they'll never let you know it.

But for an actor now, I suppose I'd say, "Come to California and try very hard to find out where the good theater groups are, or some sort of good working group. Of course, you try and find an agent. But then, it's very unfair to expect an agent to respond simply because you've walked into his office. So I would say prepare a scene—a sensible, good scene—to show agents because they do have to get excited before they can sell you. Then, I'd learn how to do a good interview. I would make it part of my stock in trade to be interesting. If they can leave an interview and I can say, "I really want to see him or her again," I'm going to bring them back to read. Also, I think the actor has to be trained to read.

His life is dependent on it. Obviously, there's no other way in television where the director has maybe five hours of his week to cast the show. That reading, that five minutes you're going to spend in front of the director and the producer with that script, is going to determine whether you're going to get the job or not. So somehow, some way, you go and learn how to read—not just how to act, but how to pick up a script, read it quickly, find a point of view about a character, and do it, and never say, "I read badly." Many times it's true—the actor who doesn't read well may be wonderful, but unfortunately, unless it's someone whose work I know and I can say to the director, "That was really a rotten reading but he's marvelous," it just isn't worth it. Once in a while the director will say, "Oh, to hell with it. We'll take a chance if Ethel's that excited about him." But that's unusual. He's got to meet a schedule; he's got to get a performance out of everyone and make the star of the series happy; and he doesn't need aggravation. So usually it's "The kid didn't read well, Ethel. I'm sorry." And that's that.

● *Do some stage actors really tighten up in front of the camera?*

I guess so. I don't know how you learn to be a film actor. You learn certain techniques; you work smaller; you don't project as much. But if you are lucky enough to have a sensible director, he'll tell you that. I suppose it's wise to take courses in film or look at yourself on tape, and that you can do in a good school. If you're basically a good actor, you make that adjustment very quickly. You sense it. But if someone's just had a classroom experience, a kind of isolated world, he would probably not be prepared to work in front of a camera.

● *What are the chances for an unknown actor or actress, once he or she has a small part on a TV show, to go further?*
It's hard to answer, because the small part can mean something or absolutely nothing. I look at film sometimes. Somebody says, "Hey, watch me on 'Bonanza' tonight," and I just couldn't tell. It was one of those wonderful parts where he's saying one line and there are a lot of actors standing around—what do I know? Sometimes you get that tiny little part and you say, "Hey, he's interesting." The good thing about it is that the director who used you may like you if you did well in a small part. The next time he does a show, he may say, "Hey, that kid, he didn't have too much to do, but I'd like to use him again." And the same thing with the casting directors. If we use a kid in a small part, we ask the director, "How did he do?" If he says, "I liked him. He was really good, enthusiastic, and I liked him," then the next time we push harder and try to get him something better.

● *If the actor produces a sort of enthusiasm and interest and has a likable personality, he's got more of a chance of making it. Right?*
Right. We can't separate ourselves, even if we try—however professional. Sometimes we say, "He's a son of a bitch, but he's wonderful." But by that time, you're talking about an established actor. When a young actor comes along, he's got to be enthusiastic, involved, on time, and he should be sitting around the set all day watching and learning. The assistant director can destroy an actor's career. "I can never find the kid. He really was a pain in the neck, Ethel. He had three lines and we spent forty minutes looking for him." And you say, "Oh, shit, I'm sorry. I won't bother with him

again." I'll find another marvelous young kid who will
sit on the stage, watching, listening, and learning. A
director senses that. Other actors sense it. Jack Lord
does that a lot. He'll say, "I love that kid. He's never
done anything before, but boy he was really right in
there, and he did well." It's hard work for the star of a
series. A series is drudgery. It's like working in a factory.
Therefore you try and make it as pleasant as possible for
them.

● *How do actors today feel about their profession? Are they
proud to be actors?*

I just think there's a whole change of attitude in the
business. If I couldn't be here, I would die. I can give up
my marriage. Send my kids away and I would go on
living, but if I couldn't work in this business, I would
die. It's my life. It's as simple as that. It has taken years
of analysis and years of facing up to the fact that this is
the one thing I cannot live without, and I honestly
don't think you should be in this business unless you
feel that way. The actors feel the worst kind of rejection
because it's personal. Every time you don't get a part,
every time you don't come back to read, then I'm
rejecting you. If it's your sonata or your painting or
something like that, you can remove yourself one step,
but when they're rejecting *you*, it's personal. God
knows, we all survive on love, and when you have to be
rejected twenty times a day or a week, it's almost
unbearable. No matter how many times you tell them
it's not personal, that the reason they didn't get the job
was because we had to have a blond or we needed
someone smaller, rejection just cannot be explained.
To them, all that happened was that somebody said,
"No." Therefore, if you don't get real joy out of acting,

if it isn't part of your life, you shouldn't do it. I don't think anyone should become an actor unless he simply cannot conceive of doing anything else.

● *You talk about the young actor being cooperative, being "gung ho." I can't imagine Brando getting in there and being "gung ho."*

I'm not talking about that. Marlon is a perfect actor. He could get up and do an exercise in class when he was seventeen or eighteen and we were mesmerized. Also, like many great artists, what must go on in his head must be overwhelming. I don't think we should talk about the great artists when we're actually discussing the young actor who's coming along. None of us can deal with the great artist. How they survive, how they live, and how they function is so miraculous, because they must feel things that most of us wouldn't ever dream about.

● *But what about those actors with talent who simply can't cope with the system?*

They shouldn't be in the business. It's just one of those tragedies, because either the talent has to be so overwhelming that it overrides all of that and surmounts it, while the little talent has to be able to deal with the realities or he will be destroyed. When you become a star, then you can do your own thing. You can't equate it with a Brando. Marlon operated on a totally different wavelength. He does walk to the sound of a different drummer. That may take fifteen to twenty years. But you hang in there because you have to.

● *Don't you believe luck has a tremendous amount to do with it?*

It does—being there at the right time. That miracle happens all the time. You're saying, "Oh, God, I really need . . ." and that kid walks in. A kid walks in and gets the job. It is luck. It's also luck if you get a little part in a film and no one sees it. It's like Broadway. The play can be a success out of town. It comes to New York and closes after one performance. Or there's the night the producer comes to see the show and says, "I need a girl that looks just like that!" It is luck. There are no rules, just some guidelines that make it a little easier.

● *Do great reviews from small theaters impress casting directors, et cetera?*

No. Many times I read great reviews in the trades, then I go to see the show. And, my God, it must have been Helen Keller who wrote that review—it was horrendous. What a review does is tell me they've worked, they're serious about their profession, and they're really trying. It's up to me to find out if they're any good. I cover less and less theater myself. My staff does it more and more for me. I can't sit through bad theater anymore. It's so painful. It's depressing and dull.

● *Do you think it has to do with the atmosphere here?*

TV and films are one step removed from the theater. They're bloodless. They're a result of forty million different techniques of work. In New York you're in contact with other actors—even in a drugstore. It's important because you are always, in a sense, in competition, but it wasn't so much competition, it was an interchange of ideas. We talked with other actors, had a sense of what was happening. Here it's lonely. What does the actor do here? He plays golf or tennis or he goes to the beach, and unless you're gay—and if you're going to be an actor, you damn well better be a fag, because there are three gay bars where they go and they talk to each other in gay bars—straight actors have nowhere to go. I love actors because they're interesting, but I think the thing that actors have to learn is that every job may be your last. You may never work again. The fact that you've had three good years does not mean that you've made it. You can go for another seven years without a job, and then suddenly you can be discovered again.

● *Is it possible to define a "star quality"?*
I think it is something that is indefinable. I think that the vaster, the more uninteresting, the more bloodless our society becomes, the less interesting the personalities are—the more individuality is put down and the individual is punished for becoming a star. It's no wonder the kids rebel today.

# Milton Katselas

## Director

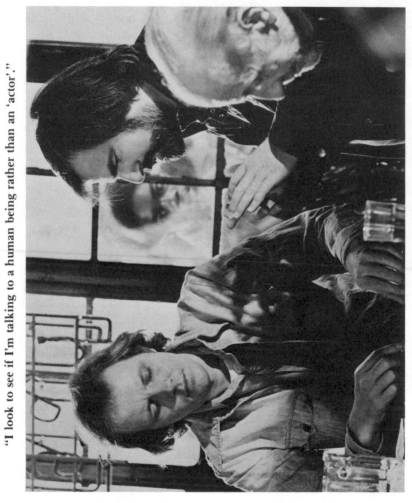

"I look to see if I'm talking to a human being rather than an 'actor'."

Directing a scene from *Report to the Commissioner.*

Milton Katselas was born in Pittsburgh, Pennsylvania, where his career as a director germinated at the drama department of Carnegie-Mellon University. From there, he headed for New York, where he won acclaim as one of the most talented young directors in the theater, directing such notable talents as Maureen Stapleton, George C. Scott, Shelley Winters, Colleen Dewhurst, Keir Dullea, and many, many others. He directed the highly successful original Broadway production of *Butterflies Are Free*. This job led him to Hollywood, where he repeated the task on film for producer Mike Frankovich. He has since gone on to direct other feature films.

Feature Films:

*Report to the Commissioner*
*Forty Carats*
*Butterflies Are Free*

Stage:

*Butterflies are Free (Broadway)*
*The Rose Tattoo (City Center Revival)*
*Camino Real (Lincoln Center Revival)*
*The Glass Menagerie (Revival)*
*Cat on a Hot Tin Roof (Revival)*
*The Zoo Story (Original Production)*
*The Price*
*Incident at Vichy*

Milton Katselas looks as if he should be living in a log cabin, chopping wood for the winter, instead of directing films in Hollywood. A handsome, rugged, bearded man, Milton is one of the new, sensitive breed of young directors, greatly respected in the industry. While making big-budget pictures for major producers such as Mike Frankovich and others, he still finds time to hold acting classes in Los Angeles. We went to visit him in class, watched how he worked, and came away impressed with his expertise and articulation. He's a man dedicated to his craft. If we were young actresses starting on a career, Milton is one of the directors we would hope to work with.

● *Are you always on the lookout to find the new, young actor or actress or do you feel more inclined to use the established actor?*

One of the most exciting things in our business is the revelation or discovery of a new talent, and the search is constant by directors, casting people, and producers to find that talent. All the great directors have always been interested in new people and have continually discovered fresh faces! How does one get there? It's a matter of a person having the talent, being persistent and being there.

● *Does luck play any part? For instance, can some people work hard, be extremely talented, and not be in the right place at the right time?*

I don't believe that luck plays any part in our lives. One can assume certain things after the fact: "Wasn't it good that I was there when . . ." and give the reasons as luck, or, "I was late for that traffic light so I just missed the plane and it crashed." This is something that is done after the fact, and I do believe, without getting too philosophical, that we do have control over our destiny, that we are the cause of our lives and what happens to us. Not luck. Every person has a different road to take, and some people are discovered quickly and easily. Others have to persist and wait their turn. Timing, you might say, is part of it, but timing is something that we can affect. In other words, an actor hears about something, tells his agent, and gets put in the running for the part. Then it's up to his talent. If I thought luck was the determining factor, I'd pack my bags and head for another planet.

● *Does the actor wanting to work professionally in film and television require training in legitimate theater?*

I don't think that a person *must* have it. I don't think

there is anything that I can conceive of in acting that a
person *must* have. I do know that the actor who's had
stage experience has learned a certain technique.
There's a discipline—not to say that there are not
undisciplined stage actors, but as a rule stage actors
learn discipline. I teach out here in Los Angeles now,
and the studio I have is ideal, but in New York the
studios where I worked were unbelievable—a bit dirty
and often hot or cold depending on the season. I loved
them, but they were just unbelievable. The life in New
York is much harder, and one has to have a certain
amount of discipline and persistence—subways, the
winter, out-of-town tryouts where you live in a hotel
room for four or five weeks—the discipline of that kind
of life can prepare the actor for the traumas, the
difficulties, and the hard work he has to go through.
But there's no *must*. No, I really don't think the film
and television actor has to have stage training.

● *When you are casting a film and someone comes in for an*
*interview, what, if anything, sparks you?*

Well, you're weighing each person that comes in in
relation to the specific project you're doing and a
specific part in that project, so you have a mental
picture of what you want. Now that picture is not just
physical, but it's also a picture of very specific
emotional attitudes and ideas. The candidate might
have a sexual quality, a certain kind of flirtation or
charm that one may be looking for in a particular part,
and yet those qualities might be all wrong for another
part. I look for the human attributes. I look to see if I'm
talking to a human being rather than an "actor," and
I'm concerned about what that human being is like and
what projects from him. In that way I myself become
the audience and view him as such.

The actor is an instrument, and things vibrate from him. The actor is the creator *and* the created thing, so what vibrations or qualities emanate from him are vital. A painter, sculptor, musician create through or on something else, so one is not concerned with what emanates from them personally. When the actor walks on a stage, without even doing any acting, certain things emanate from him. So I look to see what my response is to this person before me. Of course, I do my best to put him or her at ease, and in some circumstances perhaps I will also put him or her under a certain kind of light duress to also test how he or she reacts. But basically I'm trying to see what this person is like—his humor, his intelligence, his personality. It's not one hundred percent sure that you can succeed with this method, but these are not the first people that I'm meeting. I've met all kinds of people in my life all over the world, so although I may not be able to measure in totality that person's ability as an actor or actress simply by meeting him, I am, in a sense, relying on that interview. I'm looking to detect some aspects of that personality, something to give a clue that this is a person who could possibly do this part. There's no question that we miss sometimes. There's never that one-hundred-percent surety.

Another thing is to see can this person be a part of a group project. Can we live and work together for what is sometimes three or four months? I also try to give myself sufficient time before a production to meet all kinds of people, talk to all kinds of people, and be open to communications that may come back from the actor. For instance, if an actor feels dissatisfied with his interview, I'm open to receiving some form of communication from him saying that he thinks I missed something. Now, that might give both me and the actor another chance. Or I might have to clarify the reasons the actor's not physically right, why he or she would not satisfy my requirements, but, on the other hand, on the basis of their persistency, say, "OK, let's try it again," and proceed to explore the possibilities of this actor for the part.

● *Do you feel most directors would react the way you do to the actor that persisted in that manner?*

I believe there's a way to be persistent; there is a charm, a humor, a way to do it. I can't describe it, but again, it has to do with the actor doing it, and not luck or chance. The only shot he has is somehow to persist in getting the message to the director that he could do better if given another chance. This holds true for an interview as well as a reading. You see, I think the actor is the key to the whole thing, that the actor is the final vessel for the communication of this product we're trying to create. So he becomes, to me, the ultimate element in this interpretive art. Now I am not minimizing the writer, but the fact of the matter is that the actor is the guy who is ultimately telling the story—he's the one that has to get it across—so as far as I can see he's the most important guy in the whole thing, and if you cast your property properly you have a maximum setup to win with.

As far as interviews are concerned, some people just have an aversion to other people, and no matter what you do that actor or actress is just tight and will not respond in any way in the interview. But there must be a willingness on the part of that actor to communicate *something* of himself. Now *shy* has been the word most used as an excuse down through the ages for all

kinds of crimes, so *shy*, although it's a likable quality
and many of us respond to it more than others, is not
one of the most suitable qualities for actors either in an
interview or while performing. But it's also up to the
guy on the other side of the desk—in this case me. I've
got to be receptive enough to put him at ease enough to
pick up whether this person is physically right or get
enough of his qualities to consider him and, although I
can tell he's not good at interviews, decide that I'd better
have him in to read because it's only going to take me
five minutes and then I'll know one way or the other.

● *And how much do you rely on the reading?*

A great deal. I will read with an actor and respond to
him immediately and say, "This is the guy," and just go
with him, or I will check myself maybe four or five
times with readings and other interviews. If it's an
important part, and really every part is important, I'll
talk with him at length. Of course, if I know their work
well and respond well to them personally and they read
for the part well the first time—then that's it. But if I
don't know their work or if it's a different part from
what they generally do, I will take the time to check it
and test it. I do this in readings under certain kinds of
duress—read them for the producer, talk with them
about the part, and make sure we're on the same
wavelength so there will be no surprises.

The only time I've gotten into trouble is when I've
taken certain things for granted—having seen an
actor's work previously and not questioned him
strongly enough on the aspect that I was looking for. So
the thing cannot be left to luck or guesswork; it must be
done thoroughly and as fully as possible. I'm not averse
to meeting with actors seven or eight times to really find

231

out if they're right. I may not read them all those times, but I may improvise with them, talk to them, go to a film with them, or whatever—anything that will make me know them more, anything to make me feel my choice is right.

● *If you were a young actor starting out, what would be your course of action? What would you do?*

Each person has a different way to go, and 'it's impossible for me to put myself in the place of each actor. The routine answers, of course, are to get yourself a good teacher, find out if you need voice training, dance, gymnastic training. In other words, train your instrument and start to work in small theater so that then agents can come and see you. But basically—and this is the most difficult thing to communicate—the actor has to devise his own plan and follow his own course. For example when I was an actor and graduated from Carnegie Tech—now Carnegie-Mellon, another conglomerate—I said to the head of the school that a week after I was in New York I was going to be studying acting with Lee Strasberg and was going to be working for Elia Kazan. *Now, I had the plan.* That week I was walking in the street, and there was Elia Kazan. I chased him, went up to him, and spoke Greek. We got along, and I started working for him—taking notes and whatever else I could do for him. I also, at that time, had an interest in becoming a director. At the same time I started Strasberg's acting class. So I called the head of the school and said, "I've done it." He couldn't believe it.

The actor has to decide, has to have a plan of action and carry that plan of action out. His plan—maybe there is somebody that he admires, some director that he respects—he decides that he's going to work with that man. That decision is already fifty percent of the battle. He has to be willing to create a plan of action, to follow through with his idea or his decision. He just can't sit there and wait, can't put himself on hold, so to speak. He has to go out and try to find where he is going to make that first connection. In the meantime, he is preparing his craft by doing plays and working in theater, or he just might be lucky enough to break in immediately.

You can give actors tips about what they can do with their careers, but the actor, like anybody else, has to try and understand that it's his decision, his application of his energy, that is going to land him the job one way or another. If he's willing to take stock of himself, he will see where there are certain personal things, hostilities or otherwise, that are truly holding him back from getting along with people. When he finally meets *that* person, he has to apply himself to make that situation go right, to make it go the way *he* wants it to go. But he also has to, as I said, try to find out what is *his* road, who does he want to work with, where does he want to end up, and what are the steps that lead to accomplishing that.

The apprentice system in Europe is a very important thing, and I am amazed that more people don't take advantage of it. So few people contact directors and try to work with them, say, I'll get coffee for you. I'll run errands for you"—anything, just to be around and study the scene. A lot of people now consider themselves stars or star material and they have too much pride. You can't do that. I worked in my first year in New York apprenticing for people like Kazan,

Josh Logan, Joe Anthony, and Sanford Meisner; I
didn't even think of it as being an apprenticeship until
three or four years later when I said, "Oh, that's what I
did!" I learned more in that period about acting and
casting and what makes a real Broadway show go than I
did at school. At Tech I learned the basics of how to
direct, but there are an awful lot of other things
involved with direction than just what you learn in a
textbook. At school I did practical work. I did direct
plays, but there are more things. There are casting,
work with a writer, work with agents, actors' deals, and
so on. There are all these things that are vitally
important to know about.

There are many stories of actors who have become
"go-fers" (go for this; go for that) for directors, and
suddenly they're put in the picture or they're put in the
play. The only route not to go is the "no route" way,
just sitting back and thinking, "They'll call me." *That
doesn't work.*

● *Do you feel that some acting school classes can squash a
special quality that one might have, take away an
originality, a uniqueness?*

Again, everybody has a different route, and everybody
isn't Marlon Brando or George C. Scott. Some very
accomplished actors, George Scott being one of the
main ones, don't believe in study, don't believe you *can*
study. If I were George I wouldn't study either, because
that's his plan, his way. He did it through work,
through hard work and on his own, but I also think he
probably did study with some people, in his own way.

So the actor is primarily looking in terms of a class
to exercise himself, and if he's lucky enough to have a
teacher who'll give him some guidance as to how to

better demonstrate his talent, then he's way ahead of the game. That's almost like going to work with a good director. But talent can be corrupted in a class: of course it can. It can even happen in productions. Some people are terrible in one production and terrific in the next; part of it is casting, but also part of it is the director. I can see the acting teacher who might tell Humphrey Bogart that he has bad speech and needs to correct it. So you have to be alert to suggestions that are made by anyone—you don't just follow like sheep.

Life is a gamble, and you cannot sit there holding onto the dice and thinking, "I can't go into this situation because I might get burned; I might get hurt." You have to throw the dice, have to follow your instincts, your feelings and perception. If you're in someone's class, confidence is the best thing one can come out with—not just technique and ability to do exercises, but confidence, confidence to work, confidence to put yourself openly on the stage or in front of a camera. If you see this in a teacher, then this may be your man. If, on the other hand, you feel you want to get all your training from work, then go out there and get work, but just know something. There are no actors who are dead who are going to be successful. By that I mean you're not like a painter or a sculptor or a musician; they're not going to discover your works after you're dead. If you're an actor you have to act *now*.

Some people have more innate ability for acting than others, and certainly there are actors I have taught and worked with who have decided at a certain point that acting was not for them. Whether or not they always had that feeling of indecision we'd have to ask them individually. Maybe that's the very thing that stopped them from taking the steps that were necessary. Yet you never know when that talent is going to come to fruition. For instance, take a Geraldine Page, a Jason Robards, or a Telly Savalas and find out when they started acting, when they got their break, and so forth. Part of that break also came as a result of the fruition of their talent, not just that their talent was sitting there ready. You will find, if you do detective work, that somewhere there a change occurred in their attitude toward their work. They met some teacher; they met some director; something very profound happened which changed them and provided the juice.

● *Well, couldn't that have been that they finally got the right part that showed them off as the gifted actors they are?*
Well, that's part of it, but part of what led them to get that part is this change that I'm talking about. It rained and therefore the crops grew. It wasn't just that the crops grew; something happened in that person's life. I know, for example, that Geraldine Page, who's a tremendous actress, worked very hard in New York and got a part in *Summer and Smoke*—the best female performance I ever saw. She then proceeded to go to the Actors Studio and work in all different kinds of roles. On the basis of that, Kazan decided to work with her and did experiments and improvisations with her and worked with her on *Sweet Bird of Youth*, a totally different kind of part. I saw her do *Lady Macbeth,* and I began to think of her in all different kinds of roles. Here was a great actress, coming off of a great performance and going to class trying to grow as an actress.

So again, any cat that says this whole thing is about luck should pack his bags and go. You've got to develop your talent and your life, and when the moment comes, you'll be there to deliver. I can rattle off the names of many actors who were innately talented, never studied, achieved success, and then their careers started going down steadily. Then they really had to work like hell to get back up there. A touch of talent is not enough. It has to be nurtured. It must never stop growing.